Another damn'd, thick, square book! Always scribble, scribble, scribble! Eh! Mr. Gibbon?
– William Henry, Duke of Gloucester, upon receiving a volume of Edward Gibbon's
The Rise and Fall of the Roman Empire from the author.

I don't want to be a soldier

I don't want to go to war

I'd rather stay at home

Around the streets to roam

And live on the earnings of a lady typist.

– Anonymous World War One lyricist

David Quantick is an Emmy-winning writer and broadcaster. He has written for many TV shows (*Veep*, *The Thick Of It*, *Harry Hill's TV Burp*), radio (*The Blagger's Guide*, *One*, *Broken Arts*), and comics (*That's Because You're A Robot*). He is the author of the novels *The Mule* and *Sparks*. *How To Be A Writer* is the sequel to the chart-topping writing guide *How To Write Everything*.

David Quantick

HOW TO BE A WRITER

CONVERSATIONS WITH WRITERS ABOUT WRITING

BLOOMSBURY ACADEMIC
LONDON • NEW YORK • OXFORD • NEW DELHI • SYDNEY

BLOOMSBURY ACADEMIC
Bloomsbury Publishing Plc
50 Bedford Square, London, WC1B 3DP, UK
1385 Broadway, New York, NY 10018, USA
29 Earlsfort Terrace, Dublin 2, Ireland

BLOOMSBURY, BLOOMSBURY ACADEMIC and the Diana logo are trademarks
of Bloomsbury Publishing Plc

First published by Oberon Books
Reprinted by Bloomsbury Academic 2021 (twice)

Cover illustration by Steven Appleby
Chapter illustrations by James Illman

A catalogue record for this book is available from the British Library.

A catalog record for this book is available from the Library of Congress.

ISBN: PB: 978 1 7831 9903 7
eBook: 978 1 7831 9904 4

To find out more about our authors and books visit www.bloomsbury.com
and sign up for our newsletters.

Contents

This book is dedicated to the memory of my brilliant friend, Joss Bennathan.

INTRODUCTION

Welcome to *How To Be A Writer*, which is a kind of a sequel to my previous writing book, *How To Write Everything*. I say 'kind of' because if you claim to have written a book that tells the reader how to write everything, then you've not really left yourself much room to manoeuvre. So, to save myself the embarrassment of writing a book called *How To Write Everything 2*, which might as well be called *I Am A Liar*, I decided to write not about writing, but writers.

Writing is a process, a talent that can be improved with practise. Everyone can write, to some degree – but not everyone is a writer. There are people who write every day, and what they write affects people's lives, but they would not consider themselves writers. You can be a decision-maker or a politician or even a commentator, writing constantly, but your life and work are not defined by your writing. And you can be someone who barely composes a sentence once a year but is most definitely a writer. (Philip Larkin, for example, had a day job as a librarian, and towards the end of his life produced a new poem infrequently, but he was clearly a writer.)

The thing that differentiates someone who isn't a writer from someone who is, I would venture as bold as thunder, is this: a writer is someone whose life turns around writing like the Earth turns around the Sun. I don't mean someone who puts on a dressing gown and a little silk cap with a tassel on it and sits at a writing desk with quill pendant in hand and all that. I mean someone whose daily life, whose routines and whose calendar all revolve around the fact that they write. Writers are often people who are infected with the need to write like a vampire needs to drink blood. It sounds absurd, but if I don't write, if I don't get the ideas out – whether the idea is a full-length script or a short gag on Twitter – I don't feel well. It's got nothing to do with being visited by my muse; it's more physical than that.

A writer – a Proper Writer – is someone who doesn't just lie awake at night thinking of ways to make Act II less boring or to explain how Captain Mathers died in the conservatory (he was allergic to orchids). A writer is someone who can't stop thinking about the work they're doing and the work they're going to do. Writers often spend days in a fugue state, unconsciously assembling huge arrays of prose or dialogue and then will suddenly sit down and let it all come out in a huge but beautifully-structured torrent. Writers are at the mercy of their subconscious, which is a massive Satanic factory belching out ideas which someone has to put together and make coherent. And they're often left empty afterwards. The novelist and historian Peter Ackroyd once told me that, when he has finished writing a book, he instantly forgets everything he learned researching it. Similarly, columnists say that when they write a piece, they often have no idea of what they're going to write until they've written it.

And that's just the writing. Very few writers enjoy financial security. So a writer is also someone who lies awake at night wondering how they're going to pay their bills from a job which is, to use the deadly accurate cliché, 'famine or feast.' Writers, who are often bad financial self-managers, careen from debt to debt like overdraft-ridden pinballs, only preventing themselves from wondering where the next payment is coming from by spending the last payment on red wine. The constant pressure to earn money from a job which, for many people, is never going to be a high earner means that every day writers are forced to choose between doing work which might be emotionally and artistically satisfying but not lucrative, or doing work which is hackery but pays the bills (which is why many writers dream of being in the middle position of having hack jobs to literally buy them time to do the work they want to).

Then there's the question of organization. Very few writers have the time or the opportunity to write all day. They may have family commitments (if you work from a home that you share with other people, those people will be compelled to interrupt you because, as far as they can see, they're doing loads of chores and you're playing Scrabble on your computer) or they may find, as many writers do, that you literally cannot write all day. For a lot of writers, writing is more like a series of mad sprints than a sustained marathon. You may painstakingly craft 300 words a day or you may blurt thousands of words every morning, but either way it's unlikely that you'll do this over five or six hours. So writers worry that they're not working at the right time of day to let creativity in, they worry that they're not writing enough, and they dream of a white-painted office, possibly in a disused lighthouse, with nothing in it but a laptop and a magic pot of self-refilling coffee.

There are, super-obviously, thousands of jobs which are much harder and nastier than writing (which is another good reason to be a writer) but there are very few jobs which claw their way into your brain and constantly nag at you like writing does. Writing doesn't go away. I don't want it to go away, either, but at the same time I have to admit that it might look odd to other people seeing me walk through the park and suddenly shout, 'Yeah! That works!' and laugh like a weirdo because I've just realized that Captain Mathers was allergic to orchids.

Which is what this book is about. Understanding what a writer's life is really like. Sharing the joys and the miseries of writing for a living. And with luck enjoying it. It's called *How To Be A Writer* not because it's a guidebook for writers – I hope I wrote that with *How To Write Everything* – but because it's a book about *being* a writer, as in existing as a writer, living your life as a writer, and so on. (If I was more insistent about these things, I'd have called it *How To BE A Writer*, but that's just weird.) So this is a book about waking up in the (early hours of) the morning and remembering that you're a writer. It's about how it feels to always be worried about how you're going to make any money. It's about when you might want to do your writing, and the occasions when you feel good about what you've written.

It's based, almost entirely, on interviews with other writers. Not just to save me work (which is definitely a core aim for many writers) but because I wanted, as with *How To Write Everything*, to display the connections between different kinds of writer, to show how comedy writers and columnists and novelists and playwrights may engage in different kinds of writing but in the end are all writers and so have more things in common than not. So I've gone out and had lunch with them, or emailed them, or talked to them on the phone, and harvested years of experience and ability far beyond my own. As you race joyfully through this book, you will encounter conversations with the writer of Channel 4's *Utopia*, with two of this country's best newspaper columnists, with the author of the astonishing novel *Room*, with the writers of the most successful book parodies books of this millennium, and many other talented and knowledgeable people.

I haven't limited myself to talking to writers, though. To get something of a bigger picture, I spoke to my accountant, Catherine Rosenthal, whose knowledge of writers and their issues with money is both illuminating and entertaining. And I spoke to literary agent Jo Unwin, who knows everything about writers and was fascinatingly informative on the details of an author's life. (I did also go to lunch with my own agent, the marvellous Kate Haldane, but we forgot to do the interview. It was a very nice lunch, though.)

As far as structuring this book goes, there is a very vague attempt at rigorousness, in that the book's framework is loosely based on the notion of a day in the life of a writer, a notion it cleaves through like melted butter cleaves to a jelly.

So there we go. This book is called *How To Be A Writer*, with the emphasis on the 'Be', and it's all about writers, and it's full of writers, talking about being writers, and our first writer is –

CHAPTER ONE

JON RONSON
– 'The Fun Is When You're The Idiot'

J on Ronson is an extraordinary man. An unblinking social commentator in books like *The Psychopath Test* and *So You've Been Publicly Shamed*, his book *The Men Who Stare at Goats* was made into a movie starring George Clooney, and Jon also wrote the superb film *Frank*, loosely based on his life playing keyboards for Frank Sidebottom. He is also an excellent radio broadcaster, as I discovered when he interviewed me for an hour on his radio show about why I once hid behind a car rather than say hello to him.

Despite hiding from him (I had a hangover and wasn't feeling very chatty), I like Jon a lot. He is an unusual mixture of investigative journalist and deceptive personality writer, one of those writers who you often end up telling all your deepest secrets. Conversely, even though he writes in the first person (and, in both *Frank* and *The Men Who Stare At Goats*, has been played by Domhnall Gleeson and Ewen McGregor), in his writing Jon reveals very little about himself – other than his powerful insights into other people. He is as much a journalist as he is a personal writer: he interviews, he researches, he refines and he edits: he is The Man Who Stares at Quotes.

Jon and I met for coffee in the bar of the London hotel where he was staying on a flying visit from his home in New York and, after we had got through a weird moment when one of the hotel staff asked him to take his hat off, I began the interview at the point where I wanted this book to start – at the beginning of the writer's day.

DAVID: You're awake. What time is it and what are you thinking about?

JON: I tend to wake up between half six and seven. I used to be really superstitious. I used to think that the first four to six hours of the day from when I wake up was the only time I can write, so I can't be interrupted during that time because it's eating into my only productive time of day. But then I started to realize that's not true. I think it is true that I can only write productively for four to six hours a day, but that can be at any time during the day. So if I have to do other shit, like stuff that doesn't stress me out or tax me, if I have to do a whole bunch of that first thing in the morning and the four to six hours starts at one in the morning, that still works. It took me years to work that out, I was running to my desk at half six in the morning thinking, 'Christ, I can't waste a minute of this only time that I can work.'

DAVID: You sit down, it's seven o'clock…

JON: Well, that's when I'm at my best. I love it. I can look at a piece of writing that I did the day before and completely effortlessly know what's wrong with it and how to change around a sentence or how to move a quote from there to there. I just know how to do it. It's perfect and I feel totally like a writer.

DAVID: And you're a very clear writer. Short sentences. You're very fond of the, 'I looked at Derek. He didn't say anything.' kind of sentence.

JON: Yes, but unfortunately that clarity only lasts a few hours a day, and I'd do anything to be able to have that clarity for a few more hours a day, but I just can't.

DAVID: Are you fast when you actually write? You've obviously done a lot of preparation before you start writing.

JON: No I'm really slow. I'll turn down any type of writing where you have to write in, like, two hours. I want months. The shortest thing I write is 3000 words and there's no way that I can guarantee anybody that I can do that in less than two weeks. And that's excluding the actual interview. Let's say you interview one person for an hour and it's a 3000 word article. I really need at least a week and most often two weeks to make that 3000 words work. Do you think that's like unusually slow? Or is that about normal?

DAVID: I think I would probably take about a week. What do you do that takes so long? Do you just look at the computer?

JON: I imagine myself pompously a bit like a sculptor. For anything from a 3000 word piece to a 70,000 word book, I look at it the same way. And this is what I've been doing the last few years. I'll do all of the research, all of the interviews, so I'll go off and have the adventure – and that's sometimes just sitting down with somebody or sometimes it's getting chased by men in dark glasses, whatever it is, the actual field work – and then the first thing that I do after that is transcribe it. I always transcribe it myself, I've never sent anything out to be transcribed. It just feels like part of the process. So I'll transcribe it, but I'll never do a full transcript, I'll just listen to the bits I might use and I'll transcribe those. Once in a while I'll then go back like a couple of weeks later and listen to it again…

DAVID: So you're editing in your mind as you go. If you're leaving stuff out, you've got an idea in your mind already.

JON: Yeah, I think so. I think I have an instinct for what's boring and what's good. Also if I remember the way somebody looked when they said that or some funny joke, some little funny aside, I'll put that in bold. So then I've got like five to six thousand words, some of it's quotes from the person, some of it's my jokes and asides – and then, let's say I need to do some other research, I go to Wikipedia, and I'll put those notes in bold too to remind myself that that's not my thoughts, it's Wikipedia. And if that person says something that leads me to go off on a different journey, I'll do the same again and then I'll add that to the bottom of the piece.

So it's a mix of my thoughts and jokes, dialogue between us, independent research and other people's research. And if it's a book you maybe repeat that twenty times and then you suddenly realize you've got 150,000 words. If it's a 6000 word article you've maybe got 20,000 words, 25,000 words. I feel like the 25,000 words is like a block of marble, and then you start to chip away at it. The second part of the process is structure and narrative arc, just like a dramatist would have.

Most importantly of all, it's the whittling, it's like, 'At what point is that sentence finished?' Every morning you go back to it and you can see things that aren't working and change them. But then one morning you'll go back to it and you'll realize that that paragraph just doesn't need changing anymore, and that's when you know it's done. And when the whole thing doesn't feel like it needs changing anymore, when you're looking at it at your most clear headed at seven o'clock in the morning and you think nothing needs changing – that's when you know it's finished.

DAVID: That is what makes writing different to, particularly, film and television because a film's never really finished, it's just what you hand in. But if you're sculpting something like a human face, you don't think, 'Maybe another eye.' Your writing, when you've made it, it's done.

JON: Yeah, exactly.

DAVID: Do you ever think, 'Why didn't I say that?'

JON: Sometimes a year or two later you look back and you think, 'Five years ago I thought that was a funny joke. It's not.' And sometimes I go back to the tape six months later and realize that there was a whole thing that they said that I didn't transcribe that's actually really fucking good.

DAVID: When you're transcribing I suppose you're looking for specific things. Like you might be looking for somebody to talk about pianos and then you hear the tape and they go, 'Oh and by the way I shot my aunt.' And you're thinking, 'I didn't really get that the first time'.

JON: Like the person in the gorilla suit in the video. Have you seen it? There's a video on YouTube where they say, 'You're about to see a basketball game, and what you need to do is count the number of times the team dressed in white bounces the ball.' So you watch it and you're counting. And then at the end of the video, it says, 'Now go back and watch the video again and this time look out for the woman in the gorilla costume.' And sure enough you've missed it. A woman in a gorilla costume comes in and walks off again and you totally don't see it. It's an amazing way of showing how weirdly your brain works.

If you're writing non-fiction, it's best not to have any preconceived notions, because quite often the fun is when you're the idiot, when the thing that you thought was true turns out not to be true at all. But if you're too stick-in-the-mud about your thesis, then you might lose a whole comic narrative thing when you realize you've been a terrible twat and you aren't the world's best psychopath spotter and then the book becomes richer for that.

DAVID: Have there been moments when you stopped in midstream and realized that you weren't looking where you thought you were looking?

JON: It's always the best moment – and it's never something you can fake. In *The Psychopath Test*, I genuinely got totally drunk with my psychopath-spotting powers and I was spotting psychopaths everywhere. There was a period of time when I was completely convinced that I could spot a psychopath. I mean I know more about psychopath-spotting than other people, but my confirmation bias was going through the roof and my lust for revenge and all these other things and I wasn't noticing it. My friend

Peter said to me, 'You're losing your mind.' And when he said that I started to unpick what had been happening to me, and that made the second half of *The Psychopath Test* good. But you can't pretend to think one thing just for the comic narrative of realizing that you're wrong. It has to be authentic.

DAVID: Non-fiction is the same as fiction in that you can structure it like a novel.

JON: Good non-fiction. Some people love the other sort of non-fiction like Ben Goldacre. Ben Goldacre's thing is, 'I am an expert at this and I'm going to start my book by telling you what the book's going to be about and then I'm going to do it.' And people love that. He's smart and he's a good writer, so I'm not dissing that, but it's not for me, I much prefer to think of journalism with the structure of a movie or a fiction.

DAVID: Somebody once said, 'A story is just an explanation' and that's what your books are. 'Stay with me and we're going to find out about this together'.

JON: Mystery and not knowing something is what fuels me. Not understanding the world is like the wind behind the sails. If you understand the world I don't know how you'd write it. That's what makes Bill Bryson's *A Short History of Nearly Everything* so entertaining, because you really get the feeling that you're learning with him as he goes along. I'm quite often surprised that more people don't write in that way. There's a weird fetish amongst a lot of journalists to want to be seen as unimpeachably smart, so they don't want the joke to be on them…

DAVID: So… what's your working environment? Is it full of busts of Shakespeare or is it a blank wall?

JON: It's a blank wall. I used to be able to work in busy offices and I can't anymore. I can't even work in cafes anymore, I need total quiet. My wife goes out with the dogs for about three hours in the morning and I sit in the front room which has got a nice view of the Hudson. So the first three hours I sit where she sits, and then when she comes back with the dogs I move into this little boxy office and close the doors. For some reason I need silence. I really envied Stanley Kubrick. When I was making the documentary *Stanley Kubrick's Boxes*, his daughter said to me that he could concentrate totally, but then if somebody came in the room and interrupted him he could break concentration and chat away and then when that person left he could go back to concentrating. I can't do that at all. I need total silence and not being interrupted for those few hours when I can write with clarity.

DAVID: Fiction writers often like to play music because it affects their mood whereas I just find it gets on my nerves.

JON: And distracts you. The one thing I do do is that when I feel my brain's starting to shut down a bit, I'll maybe go on Twitter or something like that as a way to give my brain a break, get its energy back again. I do feel that a massive amount of my life is maximizing my dwindling amount of energy. I sort of think this is what death is like. But other days I'll suddenly notice that it's four in the afternoon and I've been working since seven in the morning and I've barely taken a break and I've been incredibly productive. So I think I'm probably describing the worst days to you when I'm talking about my energy sapping after two hours and I need to do something to get it back up again.

DAVID: I do that as well. I walk the dog in the park. Just being away from the working environment.

JON: That happens to me sometimes. What I'll do because I'm worried about my memory is I quite often email stuff to myself.

DAVID: Would you say that your ideas time is when you're not at your desk?

JON: No, actually I think it is when I'm at my desk. If I am out walking, I won't try and think of ideas. Has anybody that you've interviewed for this book said something that's totally surprising that's the opposite of the way you do things?

DAVID: The trivia are different. Some people play music, some people don't, some people work in the morning, some people work in the afternoon. But essentially it seems that writers work best for short periods of time early in the morning.

JON: I do think that I might have spotted a flaw in the early in the morning thing because I was so convinced for so many years that that was the case and then a few times I was unable to work first thing in the morning and I realized I worked just as well a few hours later. My view is that you definitely have a short period of time when you can work well and you think it's first thing in the morning but actually it may not be. It could be at three in the afternoon. There's just a certain amount of pressure you can put on your brain each day. It can be just as good in the afternoon. Maybe I'm wrong about that because I think everyone's a bit more sluggish in the afternoon.

DAVID: So you've worked from seven until noon. What do you generally do next?

JON: I go to the gym. By then I'm like a pent-up fucking lunatic and if I don't go to the gym I feel like I'll start shaking. It's weird but that's just the truth.

DAVID: Because your brain is overwrought?

JON: Or maybe I've just been sitting around for too long. I'll have five or six cups of coffee in that period and maybe I've been snacking a bit too. I feel totally pent up so I'll either go for a really long walk, a six or seven mile walk for two or three hours or I'll go to the gym for like an hour and forty-five minutes.

DAVID: Then what?

JON: Then there's the next problem, which is, 'What the fuck do I do now? This is the afternoon and what am I going to do? Just sit there?' So I try and think of things to do like research or admin or chores or something.

DAVID: That's the thing about being a self-employed person, it's all part of the process.

JON: Even resting, because resting is what you need to do to your brain so that you can write.

DAVID: You seem to be quite healthy.

JON: Yeah, I think that's true. I used to smoke me arse off in the Nineties. It's all to do with writing. My whole life is basically to do with work. It takes it out of me so much that I tend not to do very much in the evenings. I won't go to parties very much and I don't even really like going out for dinner with my wife, which pisses her off. Just because I'm fucked, because if you do four or five hours of concentrated writing, you're kind of fucked. And also I don't want to stay out till late because that means that I'm not going to be able to write well the next day. So you're right, I think my whole life is about work.

DAVID: I imagine if you work in a bank and you leave the desk that's it, you turn on a different switch in your head.

JON: Yeah. Also I think a lot of it's to do with whether you're an introvert or an extrovert. I think introverts probably get tired more easily. They say about extroverts that the more they socialize, the more they want to socialize. But that is the most foreign sentence I can ever imagine. I cannot imagine socializing leading me to want to socialize more. Socializing leads me to want to go home and sit alone in a room.

DAVID: Like a lot of writers, your socializing is related to work in that you go and interview people. You've met hundreds and hundreds of people, but largely with a tape recorder or with a view to extracting information from them.

JON: Also the other thing I don't mind at all is being onstage talking to an audience. I have no problem with that at all. But the signing afterwards when I have to talk to people one-on-one knackers me.

DAVID: I like being onstage but it's not socializing. When you come offstage it's still not you. People talk about your book or have you met somebody famous?

JON: Or they have their picture taken with you.

DAVID: And tell you that they're a psychopath… One of the things I wanted to talk about is that you are well known for being you as well as for writing books.

JON: Which is sort of partly my own fault because…

DAVID: Is it a hindrance to a journalist?

JON: I think it's more of a help than a hindrance. I think it's probably gained me more stories than it's lost me. It's not so much that I'm trusted as that I'm well known so people think they're talking to an important writer. And an important person is more likely to say yes to me because they see me as an important writer. It just works for me in terms of narrative and structure for it to be about me going to somebody's house. I don't know if it means I'm sort of more narcissistic than other writers.

At this point the conversation veered towards Jon's favourite singer, Randy Newman, and how he had recently re-recorded several of his old songs with some lyrics removed. As Jon had revised some of his journalism for book publication [Out of the Ordinary: True Tales of Everyday Craziness] I wondered if the two were comparable and if 'remixing' your writing was worth it.

JON: I think the bubble is sort of sacred. You're definitely in a bubble when you're writing. When I was writing *So You've Been Publicly Shamed* and *The Psychopath Test* – when I was writing all of my books, everything reminded me of what I'm working on. So I'd be in this bar and I'd see something that's relevant to my book; you're in this incredibly intense bubble and that's what writing a book is. When you're out of the bubble, you lose interest in a way sometimes. You're out of the bubble and the bubble should be sacrosanct. You shouldn't go back and reconsider it because it mattered so much in that moment.

DAVID: Peter Ackroyd told me once he's written a book he forgets all his research.

JON: That's what Lynn Barber says. You become a world expert in something for a period of time, then you just forget it all.

DAVID: Our writer's day progresses. It's the middle of the night and you wake up – are you thinking, 'What's the point of this? What have I done with my life?' And are you thinking, 'It's all right, I'm a writer,' or, 'I can do better'?

JON: Good question. Well a bit of both… I'm always surprised at how easily your confidence, it all goes. Like when I first moved to New York and I didn't really know anybody, all my confidence just drained away. I remember one time I was at my lowest ebb, standing in Riverside Park and I thought, 'I am just a man standing in a park and nothing else.' It sounds funny but it was really depressing. But then other times I think, 'Yeah, there's a body of work.' If I can get a really good talk, 600 people come. And at the very least I'll get 150 people turning up and that's pretty much any town now. So I think it shows I've got a body of work there. The fact is, you're fucking killing yourself when you're writing these books, and you're miserable, and your brain is exhausted, and you're confused and you feel like you're in a maze. The thing to remind yourself about is that if you do get it right, in a couple of years' time, someone's going to be sitting on a beach giggling at what you wrote. It's really easy to forget that when you're in your room alone for two years. It's really hard to remind yourself of that sometimes, but that is actually the truth. It is worthwhile because it is touching people, or will do if you don't fuck it up.

So there we have it. The interview does actually end at this point, not because Jon jumped to his feet and stormed out, but because I like to end interviews literally on a good line. This isn't always possible – some interviews end with an inchoate trickle into silence – but you can't beat a flourish.

CHAPTER TWO

EMMA DONOGHUE
– 'The Crazy Stitching Of The World'

Before we dive into the next stage of our writer's day, and our second interview, I want to talk about an aspect of writing that doesn't really get mentioned – largely because the people involved in it often want it kept quiet. And that is the email interview. Hundreds of years ago, all interviews were of necessity conducted face to face (all right, you could do an interview via letters but I bet nobody ever did). You might write down the replies or you might, if you had that kind of memory, recall them later but it wasn't until the invention of audio technology that interviewing really changed. The face-to-face interview was and is still the best, involving as it does an actual meeting, and the chance for the writer to observe their subject at first hand.

In recent years, however, for obvious reasons (speed, convenience), there's been an increase in interviews conducted via email. Editors don't like readers to know when an interview has taken place down the router, because they generally want readers to think that their writers have an intimate relationship with the people they interview. (I've had to write features where the magazine has asked me to at least imply heavily that I'm in the same room as the person I'm interviewing.) And also, an email interview has little or no flexibility, the answers always come over as written rather than spoken, and if the subject disagrees strongly with your line of questioning, there's no opportunity to change direction.

The following interview was conducted by email and you will see that the tone here – snappier, briefer if also lively – differs from the interview with Jon Ronson, which is not only more rambling and conversational but was also edited (by me) from a transcription (by Tommy Udo). An email interview does have the advantage for both interviewer and interviewee that the interviewee can respond at their leisure and return answers which are well thought-out, concise, and not the result of trying to think of something intelligent to say in a tearing hurry. And, as I'm sure you'll be able to guess from the tidy way the questions are phrased here compared to the incoherent bumble of my contributions to Jon Ronson's interview, while this method affords an opportunity for the interviewer to hindsight up their questions before they go into print, more importantly the email interview breeds concise answers and is the perfect venue for *l'esprit de l'escalier*.

Which is what you would expect from Emma Donoghue. An accomplished playwright and novelist, she has won an entire continent of awards, from the Irish Book Award to the Ferro-Grumley Award for Lesbian Fiction. Emma is arguably best known for her extraordinary Man Booker-shortlisted novel, *Room* (which she has also adapted for film), a book so remarkable that describing it in any way at all would spoil it. So I won't describe it, I'll just suggest that if you don't own it, you should.

Like many writers, Emma favours an early start to the day, looking forward, as she puts it, to 'That sweet moment when the kids are on the school bus that's pulling away and I can get to my computer.'

DAVID: Where do you work?

EMMA: In my home office, but sometimes when we spend a year abroad I just have a chair in a bedroom, and that works too.

DAVID: Most writers have their own individual quirks or idiosyncratic ways of working. What would you say are yours?

EMMA: I always have a few projects on the go at once, ideally contrasting (a kid's book and an adult one, or a radio play and a novel, or a historical and a contemporary piece), so each of them refreshes me to return to the other.

DAVID: I would say from my own experience that this is a good way to go. Some writers favour the monomaniac approach of working on one project and one project only, focusing on a book or a play and essentially living inside it until it's completed. Other writers, including myself, find it healthier to have projects which you can rotate, like fields, enabling you to clear your head – and also, by the way, if you're writing comedy, to use material that might not fit in your main project. On the subject of where you write – a lot of stuff is talked about the Writer's Room. Colour supplements are filled with images of antique desks upon which sit a feather that belonged to Hemingway, a signed photograph of Virginia Woolf and a stone found inside Lassie's stomach. Most writers, however, seem to agree that they can write almost anywhere, and don't need props. What is your office set-up?

EMMA: I have a regular desk on which papers pile up, a treadmill desk on which I walk for a few hours a day while working (it's ideal for email/research/editing, and not bad for writing new stuff) and a sofa on which I sit when I need to concentrate on a hard scene.

DAVID: Again, some writers use music as a background to their writing, whereas others find it destroys their concentration. What do you favour?

EMMA: Silence. I sometimes think a certain piece or style of music will help me to connect to a project, but then I belatedly realize that it finished hours ago and I didn't notice.

DAVID: Do you have distractions like pictures on your wall or games on your computer?

EMMA: Nope.

DAVID: What – if any – is your routine for the morning?

EMMA: I wish it was: write, then at the end of the day deal with pressing email. In fact it's more like: wade through all the email and other business, and domestic tasks like booking summer camps, then finally get some time to write.

DAVID: What are your interruptions, welcome or otherwise?

EMMA: Email (travel arrangements, endless drafts of contracts), which I wish I was assertive enough to ignore.

DAVID: The vague thread running through this book is the idea of a writer's day, and for me the next phase of the day is the opposite of the start. Having got oneself to the computer, it soon becomes necessary to escape from the computer. For some, ideas are generated at the desk or the computer, for others by going for a walk or entering an aikido class. And while the whole notion of 'coming up with ideas' is a grey and foggy one, it's reasonable to ask – what methods do you use to generate ideas?

EMMA: Books generate books, so what I read always gives me ideas not only for content but for style. Conversations with friends, too; gossip; travels.

DAVID: And what do you do when you're stuck?

EMMA: Work on something else – most thrillingly, notes on a future project that I'm really not meant to be working on yet.

DAVID: You've already said that you don't play games – probably the most popular way for writers to avoid doing any work in this modern jet age – so what do you do for a break?

EMMA: I might read for fifteen minutes over lunch, or occasionally go off to an afternoon film.

DAVID: One of the great disputes, in my mind if nowhere else, is the notion of writer's block. For me, there's no such thing – not because ideas flow freely through my mind at all times, but just because when something has to be written (and bills and deadlines are a wonderful encouragement in this regard), I generally find that it can be written. Do you find that writer's block exists?

EMMA: Not for me – only problems with one project, which might make me long to sneak off and work on another one. I try to harness this adulterous impulse by letting myself take a weekend or week and work on something other than what I'm officially meant to be working on; it really helps. And when I come back to the main project I sometimes see that the problems are a symptom of something wrong in my planning – for instance, if I'm bored at the prospect of drafting chapter three, I should cut that chapter.

DAVID: Writing is hard. Even when it's easy, there's still a lot of it. Everyone I know who doesn't work from home assumes we all bunk off and watch afternoon soaps. What keeps you at the computer?

EMMA: Appetite for the project.

DAVID: Probably the one question that every writer answers differently – or not – would be this one: what got you writing?

EMMA: At seven, writing a poem about fairies: the sheer pleasure of putting two words together and making something that never existed before.

DAVID: What's good about writing?

EMMA: When it's working it feels like a godlike power.

DAVID: And what's exciting about it?

EMMA: The endless variety of challenges: can I create a convincing bar fight, an original sex scene, a joke that will make readers of all stripes laugh?

DAVID: What about notes? Do you carry a notebook or anything like that?

EMMA: I have lots of little notes files on my phone, one for each project, so if I hear a good line or get an idea in the night I can put it in straight away.

DAVID: The day continues. You've done some writing, you've fought off distractions, but now it's time to deal with the bad stuff. Getting work. Writers are a curious mixture of egotist and recluse – wanting a constant stream of work but also wanting someone else to get it for them. Many writers are happy to get out there and find something to write about or someone who wants us to write, others think it's their agent's job to deal with that sort of thing. How do you get work – by yourself or through an agent?

EMMA: My agents have never generated a project for me that I can remember; they just help me shape and sell the ideas I have.

DAVID: In that case, what is an agent for?

EMMA: My primary agent gives everything I write an initial edit, and then helps me decide how I want it to reach the world; this is about who to publish (or produce or broadcast) with, as much as negotiating royalties.

DAVID: So how do you generate work?

EMMA: I welcome every apparently crazy idea that pops up in my head. And if I hear myself say, 'But I couldn't write a GENRE X,' I try to replace that with, 'Why shouldn't I try my hand at writing a GENRE X?' Best to keep yourself in the slightly-scared zone all the time.

DAVID: A common perception in many areas of life is that 'It's not what you know, it's who you know.' And while I've always been fuelled by hatred and bitterness and do sometimes feel that people are doing well because they used to be in a yacht club with the head of Channel 4, I also feel that when you do get offered work, it's because of who you are, not who you know.

EMMA: I strongly believe that in writing it's much more what you know: a really good novel by a total unknown can find its way into print and onto the bestseller lists. It's not about which cocktail parties you're seen at.

DAVID: Talking about which – it's lunchtime. Do you have lunch out with your media chums, are you spending time with your family, or are you eating a sandwich at your desk?

EMMA: A quick bite with my partner if she's home and otherwise reading, either for the project or for pleasure.

DAVID: And how do you organize your breaks? Are you a 'Can't stop! I'm on a roll!' person or a long distance runner who paces yourself?

EMMA: I have to stop at 4.25pm when I run for the school bus. If the kids have a class in the evening I always whip out my laptop there and enjoy another hour or so of work.

Now shades of evening seep into the afternoon, bringing with them fresh dread and melancholy. Or rather, the self-employed person's panic about money.

I cannot emphasize enough (writerspeak for I can't remember if I mentioned this before but I can justify repeating myself by saying that it's important) how much money crowds out other thoughts when you're self-employed. There is no safety net. You constantly take on too much work just so you can reassure yourself that you're making money. You even, insanely, take on unpaid work because 'it might lead to something.' Even when you're clearly making a reasonable living from writing, you can't get out of the habit of worrying where your next meal is coming from.

Money consumes writers' brains. So try, at least, to control it. Don't let it make you cry. Do your accounts. And so on…

DAVID: How do you deal with your finances?

EMMA: I find money utterly tedious and grudge every minute spent doing accounts.

DAVID: Do you live in fear of penury and debt?

EMMA: I must sheepishly admit: no.

DAVID: Have you ever been poor and lived in a proverbial attic?

EMMA: Well, twenty years ago I was a graduate student in one room in a housing co-op, so fairly poor but never scared by it, because I didn't have anyone to support back then. Also, I've always written quite a lot, and in a variety of genres, so one kind of writing (typically my fiction sales in the US) supported others (my theatre work, which has never earned me much).

DAVID: Knowing what you know now, how would you advise a newcomer to the world of writing to proceed financially?

EMMA: If you have dependents or high rent and need a regular income, don't give up the day job, because many a great novel has been written in evenings and weekends.

And now a moment of contrast. Evening shades turn to the glitter of night. Moonlight, neon, flash bulbs. Success! Quite possibly.

DAVID: What is your personal definition of success?

EMMA: Getting to write the things that obsess me, and having those plays and books reach other people.

DAVID: And what is your personal definition of success?

EMMA: It's never happened, but I suspect if I put my heart into a book and then couldn't find anyone in the world to publish it, I'd feel I'd failed.

DAVID: Are you a perfectionist or a 'That'll do' kind of person?

EMMA: Well, not neurotically perfectionist, but I do like to redraft and redraft and redraft.

DAVID: Let's take a moment to talk about reviews and criticism. What's a damning criticism to you?

EMMA: My first novel got one review that said, 'Her heroine has a lot to say but none of it is very interesting.'

DAVID: And have you ever been damned with faint praise?

EMMA: Of my historical novels: 'It was very educational.'

DAVID: Writers have widely varying opinions of critics. Some regard them as parasites who can't write novels and plays so shouldn't be allowed to review them, while others actually find critics' comments occasionally useful. Where do you stand?

EMMA: They're highly useful, and I'm appalled at the erosion of their profession and its replacement with reader reviews on Amazon.

DAVID: What about friends and family? Do you value their opinions?

EMMA: I think it's unwise to ask for editorial input from loved ones because it hurts too much if they don't like it.

DAVID: All published writers have their work filtered, criticized and probably improved by editors. Do you like editors or do you find them a hindrance?

EMMA: Oh yeah, they're on my side: I have three editors (New York, Toronto, and London) for most books I write and I relish rewriting in response to their suggestions.

DAVID: As well as a novelist, you're also a playwright. Two kinds of writing with very different attitudes to collaboration – so to what extent does collaboration occur in your work? Do you like directors?

EMMA: If I had to pick one genre it would be fiction because there I'm boss... but I get so energized and excited by my collaborative times with theatre or film directors… and then I rush back to fiction again with a certain relief afterwards.

And now a moment of relaxation, or not. Given that for many people taking a break from writing is a Canute-like act of futility – if you stop writing, the writing you haven't done just laps at your feet until you have to deal with it again – it's unclear whether writers can ever really take a break. But then, parties are nice, and dinners, and winning things… And then there's television, and music… and sleep… But for many writers, writing gets everywhere.

DAVID: Is writing literally your life?

EMMA: Well, it's the biggest bit, but my partner and kids are another big chunk, and friends matter too. No important hobbies though.

DAVID: Is it just your livelihood or more than your livelihood?

EMMA: A vocation, definitely; I'd do it even if I'd never made a penny from it.

DAVID: How do you deal with free time?

EMMA: I enjoy high-quality TV drama on the couch with my beloved in the evenings.

DAVID: Do you partition off work from the rest of your life?

EMMA: Well, I don't walk away from dinner parties or cuddles with my kids to work on the novel… but I do jot things down in my phone, so I'd have to admit that the books are always hovering in the back of my mind.

DAVID: What about holidays?

EMMA: I'd prefer not to; my ideal day would always include a few hours of writing. But sometimes when travelling with the kids I have to take a couple of weeks off.

DAVID: Other people clearly have demands on your time – do you welcome these demands?

EMMA: Like every parent I have my gritted-teeth moments, and I'd buy an I'D RATHER BE WRITING bumper sticker if it wouldn't hurt the kids' feelings.

DAVID: So… what is fun for you?

EMMA: Dreaming up a new book; staying in the library so long I forget to eat or pee; giving public readings and hamming up the accents.

DAVID: And what is hell?

EMMA: Contract negotiations!!!

I've always enjoyed the scene in Stephen King's Misery *when the author finished his new book and celebrates with a cigarette and a whisky. I imagine real-life writers have such rituals, although – in the interests of balance – I also suspect several writers just push their manuscript aside and then go and watch television instead.*

The problem with endings is that they often don't exist. I've worked on television shows where the edit never seems to end, and lines are being added in post-production. Films come out in so many versions and cuts that the idea of a definitive edit is highly contentious. Books at least have a certain consistency in that authors do tend to let go once it's at the printers. But writing 'The End' at the end of a script or book is often more hopeful than definitive.

DAVID: Do you have any finishing rituals?

EMMA: No, by that afternoon I'd be working on something else. It's like gardening; there's always something that needs doing.

DAVID: Any rituals of any kind?

EMMA: When the first printed copy arrives, I kiss it; that's about all. Oh, and I make up bad reviews of everything I write just before it reaches the public, to amuse my partner but also to superstitiously ward off disaster.

DAVID: Does a piece of work ever really end?

EMMA: I always feel a pang when I send the corrected proofs off, because they contain sentences that are no good but it's too late to do anything about it.

DAVID: Do you want to grab the work back from the person making it public?

EMMA: I did try to pull my first novel before publication because I felt my second (which I'd sold with it, as a package) was stronger, but the editor told me many people would prefer my first, and she was quite right. No, apart from that I've always been thrilled by that moment of going public, though nervous too.

And finally… the wee wee hours. The working day has ended, the loved ones are in bed, and it's just you, the writer, still awake, full of doubts. Why am I doing this? What's the point? I'm going to starve aren't I?

And then the sun rises on a new day…

DAVID: What makes you doubt what you do?

EMMA: Nothing: it's what I'm here for.

DAVID: And what makes you think you might be good?

EMMA: I try not to think about me and how good or bad I am, more about the story that's burning for someone to tell it (and it might as well be me).

DAVID: What do you want from the future?

EMMA: To live long enough that I can get out all the stories in me.

DAVID: How would you justify your life to some sort of weird supernatural court?

EMMA: It does occur to me that it's less directly good for the world than being a doctor, say, but hey, you have to play to your strengths.

DAVID: And finally… what are writers for?

EMMA: Making a meaningful pattern out of the crazy stitching of the world.

Which is a great way to end an interview, so I'll leave Emma here and say thank you.

CHAPTER THREE

SUZANNE MOORE
– 'I Kind Of Eavesdrop A Lot'

I have, as I say, attempted to structure this book, and sometimes this plan works, but from time to time it doesn't. This chapter would be an example of my structure not working, because it is an interview with someone who manages to be incredibly disciplined without giving the least impression of being disciplined. She is, by and large, a columnist for newspapers and periodicals, and has the great columnist's genius for finding the clearest path, the strongest argument and the most powerful conclusion without at any time making you think that you are reading an essay or being told anything.

She is Suzanne Moore, and she is quite possibly the brainiest person I have ever met; so brainy that she makes me nervous, as if she were a mad scientist (I should point out that she is neither a scientist nor mad). Suzanne has written for *The Guardian*, *The Mail On Sunday*, *Marxism Today* and *The New Statesman*. Her columns sometimes inspire controversy but more usually they inspire thoughtfulness, clarity and entertainment. Columnists are a popular feature of modern publishing, from blogs to magazines. In a world where everyone has an opinion and they plan to staple it to your face, a good columnist, full of intelligence, opinion and even fact, is increasingly hard to find. Suzanne Moore is definitely one of the best. She is able to write columns that are full of her personality and own view of life that aren't empty rants, and she also has the ability – rare in the field – to back up her points with information and research. She's also a great person to sit next to in a champagne bar. I know this because we met for this interview at a champagne bar on St Pancras station. It was handy for both our journeys home and they do wine. Suzanne began our conversation by telling me that, effectively, I was wasting my time talking to her.

DAVID: So you say you don't have anything useful to impart...

SUZANNE: Don't say that! Because I teach a masterclass at *The Guardian*, so I have to pretend to have something to say.

DAVID: All right, let's talk about the theme of this book, which is loosely based around a writer's day. For example, when do you get up and start writing? Is there a normal time?

SUZANNE: Yeah, but that's just to do with getting my daughter off to school. I get her up at quarter past seven. If I didn't have any responsibilities I would never get up. I would stay up very late at night. I always envy people who get up early and seem to write loads in the morning. When you read those *Secret of Success books*, that seems to be what they all do. They get up at five a.m., do 2000 words and then have a nice lunch.

DAVID: I always blame Margaret Thatcher, who used to say that she only needed three hours of sleep a night...

SUZANNE: The idea that you don't need sleep is disgusting.

DAVID: Do you do normal things before you do any writing?

SUZANNE: Well, I'm at home and everyone who works at home has something to do that could potentially be called work, even though it obviously isn't work. I say, 'I want to' a lot. 'I want to watch TV programmes or listen to the radio…' Or, 'I need to…. I need to do this.' Go away, I say to my children, I need to be reading *OK* magazine. They say it as well, they've got it from me. They say, 'I need to watch the Kardashians'.

For me, there's not a proper boundary between what is and isn't work. I think it's really common. I have a thing where, before I'm about to write a column, I've got no idea what I'm going to write. I never know what I'm going to write, I never know what I'm going to do, most of the time. But there is something that is going on in the background of my head. It must be. That's all I know. I don't mean it in a mystical way, but certain things are whirring and I just have to trust that that will happen.

If I go on holiday for a few weeks, I never ever know if I'll be able to do it again. I've never thought of it as anything more than a temporary job, and I've always thought that perhaps one day it would be something I couldn't do. That sounds like I'm in a constant anxiety about it but I'm not. Simply because I've been doing it a long time, I know that by tomorrow night there will be something online at *The Guardian* by me. I can't tell you what happens in-between. I know it will happen, because it's happened a lot but if I stop for a bit I just think, 'How will I start again?' Do you worry?

DAVID: I worry all the time about what's going to happen next. I think being a freelance writer is a permanent headache and in your mind there is constantly an image of an abyss, into which you are about to tumble.

SUZANNE: I am freelance, I don't get holiday pay, I don't get anything like that… But I think it has to be that way. Maybe that's a cliché but perhaps you do need a certain amount of stress to do it. If I didn't have a deadline I just wouldn't do anything. I think I can deal with almost anything with a deadline. I was one of those children at school who really annoyed everybody because I hardly went to school. My mother didn't care about schools and I just didn't have to go. But I loved exams. That was really annoying to my friends, because I just did nothing and then went, 'Great, exams!'

DAVID: Do you think exams are a kind of preparation for deadlines?

SUZANNE: Yeah. It's an intense regurgitation of stuff.

DAVID: The nearest I've got to the way I think you work as a columnist is if I'm asked to go on a topical radio show and I have to write a column about something that's happened that week. So when they call me up and ask me to think about what I want to write, I'm not thinking of topics, but I do start being aware of topics. I see patterns.

SUZANNE: That's quite corny, isn't it? When I do those little memoir things for the *New Statesman*, they're very filmic to me and I see them. One of the things when I do those masterclass things is I tell everyone – and they really hate this when I tell them, especially anyone under thirty who wants to be a columnist and write the kind of stuff I do – is, 'Don't wear headphones in public.' And it really annoys them when I tell them that. But public opinion isn't something that comes out of the ether, or is given out by *The Guardian* and the BBC. Public opinion is when you see a fight on a bus between someone who's got a pushchair and someone who's in a wheelchair. Or I'm in the school playground and some mum says, 'Oh, I quite like that David Cameron.' That's how you know what's going on, way more than anything I read in the newspapers. It's a kind of instinct. You just have to listen. So if you go around plugged into headphones... I can tell exactly who does that because every column they write, the only ordinary person they've ever met is a taxi driver. I can be like that just as much as anyone, I'm not trying to say I'm down with the people, I'm just saying you have to listen to what's going on. I kind of eavesdrop a lot.

DAVID: Can you remember anything you've heard that may have been a starting point for something?

SUZANNE: It's usually political, like a mood or how people are talking in the pub or the playground... I mean, take the last election. Most people got that wrong, which I think was a real lesson to journalists about what you should do and what you shouldn't do. I mean, I got it wrong but the bits I didn't get wrong were where I'd gone and spoken to people, really old fashioned reporting. I'd gone down to Thanet, I know Thanet well, and spoken to UKIP people. It was obvious to me that at the end of the day, they weren't going to vote UKIP, they were going to go in there and vote Tory, or they weren't registered to vote. And also their feelings around that stuff are really complicated, they're not all terrible racists, they're just mixed up with all sorts of things. Anyway, listening to those people I knew Farage wasn't going to get in.... Then there's just all the reading that you do around it. I read. I just read and read and read. There's no shortcut.

DAVID: What do you read?

SUZANNE: Well, now that we've got the bloody internet giving us links every two seconds there's so much more stuff to read.

DAVID: You go on Facebook and everyone's a columnist.

SUZANNE: Years ago one of the tabloids wanted a column, and the editor said, 'We've got more fucking columns than a Greek temple!' It's true. I call it TripAdvisor criticism. If everyone thinks that their opinion is valid and equally valid, you don't have professional critics anymore and you don't have music critics or film critics. This is not new. When I was at *The Independent*, they were pressing down from above to cut costs, and the first things that go are foreign news, and then they say things like, 'You don't need an art critic, you don't need music critics, anyone can do that, anyone can go in a gallery and say if it's good or bad.' It's a refusal to see that some people have honed a skill and it's really, really sad. TripAdvisor criticism is now what a lot of journalism is…

It's like if you get an Uber cab, you're meant to rate the driver. In so many areas, you're meant to rate your experience the whole time, so people think that they are critics. It's this insane thing that everybody's opinion is equal. I know I'm meant to be a socialist and say it's democracy, but everyone's opinion isn't equal, it isn't. And that's why you can't read two hundred contradictory things on TripAdvisor, because in the end you say, 'I'm going to that hotel, it'll be fine'. Because if you get into that mind-set …

DAVID: … you end up counting the reviews. 'There's thirty-eight for and thirty-six against. I'll go, then.' You send someone to see a film and it's a remake of a French film.

'How does it compare to the original?' 'I don't know, I haven't seen the original because I'm not a real film critic.' Somebody that's been a film critic for twenty years is probably better at it than someone who's been doing it since Tuesday.

SUZANNE: Yeah, that's it. If you try to write without a bit of knowledge then… More and more people are encouraged to give an opinion without having any evidence other than, 'This is how I feel.' But it's hard to say to any young person who wants to be a writer that you need more than just a style, you need to get out there and do a few things and then worry later on. Obviously you're not going to have experience and authority when you start, so you can't say, 'That's what you need to be a writer,' because that would mean that no one could ever start. I'm just trying to talk about the value of those things and your own confidence. One of the things that I would say to anyone who wants to do it – and I don't even know if it happens any more – is that good editors are like mentors and they tell you, 'That was good that piece, that wasn't great, you didn't do your best.'

I was a film critic and I used to work with this woman at *The New Statesman*, and she was so hard on me. I came to really like her and respect her but the most praise she would ever give me was, 'I quite liked that.' And all I did was want to please her, and actually she was brilliant for me. She was always really backing me and supporting me. But she never did that gushing thing. And some weeks she would say, 'Well it wasn't a good week, was it?' Which is true, it happens. Now, because everything is put online so quickly without much editing, I don't think people get the feedback. I went months last year without speaking to anyone at *The Guardian*, I just wrote it and they stuck it in. It's just as well I can do it. Maybe I can't do it!

DAVID: You'd know if people didn't like it. There wouldn't be any retweets.

SUZANNE: That's all there is now. That's it. And the inevitable upset of things you can't anticipate.

DAVID: I sometimes think there should be a test that you have to pass before you're allowed on Facebook.

SUZANNE: On Twitter, it's just people screaming at each other.

DAVID: I would just be terrified to do your job to be honest.

SUZANNE: It's got worse, this comments stuff. It's hard to take. I know you're meant to say, 'I'm so tough, I don't care,' and most of the time I don't. If I actually read a lot of it, I would never write another thing. It's just so negative. Today I wrote a really not very controversial piece on tipping waiters, saying, 'Why don't we pay people properly or tip properly?' which doesn't seem to me to be that controversial, a kind of obvious column. The comments are all, 'Why should we tip people? They just carry plates.' No idea that…Ugh.

DAVID: Let's say somebody's gone mad and they're sixteen and they want to be a columnist – how is that different to when you started? You'd have a column once a week, in a paper that was actually made of paper and instead of a daily tsunami of comments, you might get a letter or two. What was the world like when you started delivering columns?

SUZANNE: I do feel like that. I am nearly ninety… The other day I was talking with someone about the horrible abuse and death threats that you get, particularly women, and then I found myself doing that *Monty Python* thing of, 'you tell that to young people nowadays…' I was talking about when I had a real proper death threat, in the form of letters – I did used to get them at the *Mail*, Combat 18, the fascist group, had my phone number and they started ringing me up saying that they weren't going to kill me, they were just going to disable me. I have to say the police were good, the *Mail* was good, everybody took this very seriously… And then I got a message of support from Norman Tebbit because he was also at the *Mail* – which is worse for me politically than the actual death threat. He was saying, 'You're nothing until you've had a death threat.' And it was quite sweet really, except it's Norman Tebbit, which kind of did my head in because…

DAVID: Did you reply?

SUZANNE: I don't even remember. The point is I used to get actual letters and I still do get actual letters and I'm always quite touched. At the *Mail* I used to get those little floral notelets that you used to buy your auntie, little pretty cards in an envelope, a nice little floral card in a nice little lavender envelope, and I used to open it up and it just used to say 'Cunt!' I wish I'd kept them now, I could put them in some kind of installation of hate mail.

DAVID: Back to the advice thing…

SUZANNE: I would say to anyone who wanted to be a columnist is that it's really good to start writing regularly and have a specialism. I don't think this idea that everyone can do everything equally is true. Some people are really good at interviews, some people are really good at columns and some people aren't. I could do ten columns in the time it would take me to do an interview, I find that a lot of work. I talked to (legendary interviewer) Lyn Barber and she said, 'I don't know how you do that.' I don't know how she does what she does. I don't know how she's interested in half of these people. But she is, she genuinely is.

DAVID: I think people admire a columnist work-wise because they seem to be so good at generating ideas.

SUZANNE: Yeah. I wish someone fed me ideas, but they don't. If I ask them at *The Guardian*, 'What have I got to do this week?', they just say, 'Syria.' I mean that's not an idea, is it? 'Syria', or 'Youth', or 'Violence.' They just say these really vague things that aren't ideas. Also when I write any kind of an opinion thing, it has to be an idea that works for me. When I've tried to do things for people that I don't really care about… I just can't do it. Not because I have all this integrity or something like that, it just doesn't work. You have to work yourself up. So even though I don't care about anything now, by tomorrow morning I will be incensed by something or other, because that's how it works.

DAVID: So if I said to you ten days ago, 'What do you think about tipping?' Would you say, 'I don't care'?

SUZANNE: No tipping? Well, I would have an opinion just because I've been a waitress, but… there's been a recent news story about a charity where I would have said that that's what's whirring in my mind at the moment, and I know I may end up writing about that because I'm kind of fascinated by the fallout of that story. And also because I've always heard all the rumours… But I don't know if

I'll do that tomorrow, and I feel like I might upset too many people with that one.

The advantage of doing what I do is when you get it right it's a big buzz. On Mondays I have to do something called First Thoughts, which is just my reaction and it doesn't have to be as formed as a column. I was on the phone and they were about do the deal today on the Greek economy, and my editor said, 'I don't think it's going to be until this afternoon, what else do you want to do?' and she said she'd call me in ten minutes when she got off the train. And in that ten minutes, the deal was announced and I had a first go at that piece. And that's great if you just go and you get it right. And you get it right because you will have been reading for weeks about it. You don't get it right because you just decide that day, you need to keep following all the big stories. But I've just done a couple of festivals and I've had no internet for days, so I don't know any news.

DAVID: How did that make you feel?

SUZANNE: Everything just carries on without you. And then you come back and you can catch up. It made me realize how ridiculously hooked into that news cycle thing I am and that it's perfectly OK to switch off for a minute. Most of my friends don't read the news because they find it depressing. I'm the opposite. I hardly watch any TV that isn't news.

DAVID: So you're not massively interested in the Kardashians?

SUZANNE: I've only seen that recently for the first time. I'm not really driven by fiction or drama. I like real things.

DAVID: I've noticed that there's a real divide between people who read fiction and people who read non-fiction.

SUZANNE: I've been to see some publishers recently and I realize that non-fiction is the only thing that lots of men read, they just don't read fiction. I didn't realize how gender-based it is, I really didn't. I just had to judge a book prize and I was really struck by how much better the non-fiction was than the fiction. For me. I think it's just to do with age. I haven't got time for this made up stuff. And I read a lot more American journalism.

DAVID: Is that still a place where British journalism and publishing take a lead from?

SUZANNE: I think so, I don't know. *The Guardian Daily* now does this Long Reads thing, which is a long essay, 5000-6000 words, and a slightly American *New Yorker* kind of idea. It's counter-intuitive in this time of the quick tweet. People actually do want a long solid read. It takes quite a long time to read some of those pieces, and some are worth it and some aren't worth it. But for me, everything is always about – this is terrible – 'Write as few words as possible for as much money as possible.'

DAVID: Apart from the money, what are the reasons for that?

SUZANNE: Because I've done a tabloid column and they're shorter, and everyone always assumes that they're easier to do than a long column, and that's just not true. It's much harder. I was doing two 1500 word columns a week, which I now think is insane, because who wants that much? It's mad. But now at the *Guardian*, my column is 900 words and I think, 'Well, if you can't get it out in about 1000 words…' You should be able to do it. But in my head there are all different structures of what 500 words looks like, what 700 words looks like, what 1200 words looks like. This is just experience. And sometimes an editor will say, 'How much do you think you can do on that?' and I always go for the absolute minimum that I can do. Sometimes I'll go to 2000 words or something. I quite like the wham bam nature of journalism. I do like the fact that it's so quick. I still get a hit from that. When you write books, how long do you have to wait before anyone retweets you?

DAVID: Years. I think working for the trendy papers is different from the places I write. You write something for *The Telegraph* and it's three days before anyone retweets it.

SUZANNE: But even before the internet I did the thing where you write it and it's in the paper the next day, that's it. It doesn't have to be perfect because it never is going to be. There's something about the speed of it I like. There's something really liberating. You have to say to young journalists, 'You know what? You might get it wrong, but the next day no one will remember that and you're onto the next thing.' That helps you to be freer in what you say. It doesn't have to last forever.

Good columns do last and they're meaningful sometime later but they don't have to be. You're not having the last word on everything all the time. Certain subjects you come back to again and again and you know that you've got something with that thing. But there are things you just get wrong. And if you've got them wrong in a book…

DAVID: It's newspapers, it's not the *Encyclopaedia Britannica*.

SUZANNE: And one of the things that's really changed is that sometimes you get stuff wrong, sometimes the subs get stuff wrong… I'm not blaming the subs, but there can be a mistake in a column that four or five different people have looked at – especially with figures, a decimal point in the wrong place, something like that – everyone's looked at it, and it goes online and instantly everybody's telling you that you're wrong. You just have to correct everything instantly and just apologize.

DAVID: The singer Morrissey sued me. Who's had a go at you?

SUZANNE: Hugh Hefner tried to sue me for saying that he was a pimp and his girlfriends were prostitutes. Russell Brand for saying his stuff is ghost-written. Nadine Dorries, who complained about a quote that she had given to the *Daily Mail*. The libel itself that I did against her was her own words. But the biggest trouble I ever got in, legally, was… somebody had sex with a dolphin and there was a court case and it went sub judice (i.e. it can't be discussed publically). So I wrote a really silly, stupid column about whether this dolphin had been basically asking for it and all of that sort of thing. It was stupid, I don't know how I did this. Was it swimming about looking sexy? All of that. Anyway the judge in the trial went bloody mad, they could have had to dismiss the jurors in this trial of this man who had sex with this dolphin.

DAVID: I feel we've strayed, but in a good way. Can we talk about writers as opposed to writer's bosses? When I was at *NME* I used to think I wanted to be the editor because I thought that was the ultimate writing job. Then I realized editors weren't the kings of writers, they were publishing administrators.

SUZANNE: It is a powerful job.

DAVID: Not many writers are interested in power, are they?

SUZANNE: We're not writers now, we're content providers. But when I get really worried about all this stuff, I think that the rise of the columnist and the individual voice is a reaction to that content thing, because people are bewildered by how much stuff is there and look for certain people to work them through it. That's what some columnists do.

DAVID: Columnists are filters. They say, 'Let's have a think about what you think.'

SUZANNE: Sometimes a column is you verbalizing what someone would say if they had the time to sit down and say it, and sometimes it's you pushing the reader, or making them say, 'She is completely wrong.' Sometimes the most obvious columns are not the most interesting to write because we all know what we think. Actually, the more interesting thing to write is something where you don't know yourself where you're going to go with it. I can't say, 'Well, I'm going to say this, I'm going to make point A and point B.' I know that something will interest me and it will come out if it's a good idea. If it's a bad idea, I will be bored so I'll have to do something else, so I'll ring them up and say I can't do it.

DAVID: Do you ever abandon columns?

SUZANNE: Very occasionally. You should go with your gut thing – the thing that you keep coming back to. The thing you hear people talking about in the pub will be the idea that you should do. Sometimes you think, 'I can't write anything about that, because ten other people have written stuff about that,' but actually your readers won't have read every other thing about it, so you can have a go at it.

DAVID: And I think people read your columns because it's you.

SUZANNE: I used to think – and this goes back to the thing you asked me about being really old because it goes back to the pre-internet days – it was one of the things where people had a relationship with you. Like we used to write letters to each other, people would communicate to each other in writing and would feel there were certain people that they knew and that they trusted. But I always get asked about which columnists I like. I do read all the opposite people to me, the right-wing ones, and I do like some of them. There's a lot of rubbish though.

DAVID: Sometimes columns seem to be written by an anonymous man on a generic topic and it's a plod through verbal porridge full of phrases like 'On the other hand' and 'But then again.'

SUZANNE: Well there's too much of that – as a woman, I was always asked to do loads of interviews and stuff and I used to say, 'No, I don't want to do that, I'm not interested in actors, they never say anything,' and they used to say to me, 'What do you mean? You're a people person.' What does that mean? It means that you can't think. It means that women feel and react to people doing interviews and men do pieces about the state of the economy and who we should have as a government. That still goes on. There *are* more women up there – we've now got thousands of those, 'I hate myself, I'm twenty-six,' kind of women. There's millions of those confessional things. Blokes do them too but…

DAVID: You never get a column from a man saying, 'I cried for three days without stopping…'

SUZANNE: You could do that column.

DAVID: If you go on Twitter and say something nasty, some people like it but most people don't. If you say something nice, people love it. If you say, 'I cried,' people go mad. People get really happy and say, 'Well done you.' It would be a good column actually. The man who cried.

SUZANNE: Yeah. What I meant was the idea that writing is feeling and not thinking, I mean, it's obviously both. That's the difference between a column like what I do and that thing they have in *The Guardian Weekend* where it's all, 'I was swallowed by a shark', mad experiences that grab you because they're just these strange experiences. But if you said to that person who was swallowed by a shark, 'Do this every week', they couldn't sustain it.

You have to be able to sustain it. My neighbours come up to me often in the street and say, 'You know, I could be a columnist, what do you think? Have you got ten minutes to tell me how to do it?' I don't think they realize that it's a bit insulting. I wouldn't go up to them and say, 'Oh you're a doctor, I think I could do that,' or 'I want to be an interior designer, have you got ten minutes to spare?' But they do it all the time. It's like that thing, 'Everyone's got a novel inside them, and that's where it should stay.' Everyone has between three and six columns inside them, things that they feel very strongly about and think they could produce something on. But they haven't got ten years' worth.

DAVID: Is it all about generating ideas?

SUZANNE: That's the thing you are paid for really. The actual writing isn't the work. That's quite quick. It seems like you get paid a lot for not doing very much, but it's the rest of it. It sounds so wanky, but it is to do with reading a lot and trying to understand things.

DAVID: Generating ideas as opposed to having ideas is hard work. I know this from comedy writing. A sitcom is easier because you only have one idea, but a sketch show is crippling because you have to come up with thirty ideas for half an hour. Obviously writing columns exercises your brain and enables you to work out how to have ideas.

SUZANNE: Everything is material potentially, but that doesn't mean anything is. You learn when something is an idea and something isn't. You learn how to do it by trying to write things that aren't very good ideas and you have to say, shit, this isn't a good idea... But everybody writes differently. I never rewrite anything and if I have to, that means it's gone wrong and I probably have to abandon it. I don't think my way is better or worse, I just know that's how it is for me.

DAVID: But you do have an ability to structure.

SUZANNE: Structure is really important to me. Structure's everything, first line, last line, it's absolutely, 'Bang bang bang, punch punch punch.' I think that's to do with having done a tabloid thing where you have to do it in a short space. If you have 1500 words, you can walk somebody around an argument, you can go off on a bit of a reverie and come back. But if you have 600 words, you're 'Bang bang bang.' There's not much subtlety there but it's quite hard to do.

Structure's everything, but when I try to explain structure in classes, I looked at my own notes, I couldn't explain it. I think the structure really will come out of you if it's the right idea. The other thing that I say to people – because my job is to put them off, put them off trying to do my job. The first time I ever did one, Marina Hyde was there in the morning. I got there in the afternoon and all those people were running around saying, 'Whatever you say to these people, please please don't depress them!' Marina had just said to this audience of *Guardian* readers who had paid hundreds of pounds to see her: 'Forget it. There are no jobs.'

But the one thing I do say to people, which is one of the things people don't understand about writing, is that if you really can't stand to be on your own a lot of the time then you're not going to be a writer. People imagine a bustling newspaper office or – I don't know what they think writing is, but they don't think of sitting in on your own. And that is what it is. If you are someone who needs to be with other people all the time, I don't think you're going to be a writer. And I say that to people and they look a bit crestfallen.

DAVID: It's a passport to loneliness, even if you do like being on your own.

SUZANNE: You have to be on your own to do it and you have to try to build other events in your life where you're sociable otherwise you will be on your own. But if you can't stand your own company, I don't think you're going to be a writer. The fantasy of what a writer *is* is still someone who is always fantastically social. You can be social sometimes but it isn't a social process, it's quite anti-social really.

DAVID: People who don't write always seem to say to me, 'Oh, if I was on my own all day I'd just watch daytime television.' You wouldn't do that because you'd starve to death. You're the first person I've spoken to who's talked about the anti-social nature of writing. If you live on your own you look out the window and suddenly it's dark and you have no lights on in your home… you've just been looking at a screen all day.

SUZANNE: You asked me about my day – tomorrow morning I don't have to get a child off to school but I'll get up and have a couple of hours milling around. I now understand that a lot of the things I do before I start writing are part of it and I can't stop it. I will do anything but write, I will do housework, I will suddenly think I need to go and buy a red pepper… One of the things I have to do – and this makes me sound like a psycho – I have to get dressed and put some lipstick on, like I was going to work. Otherwise it's really bad, I'm just in bed on my laptop. I get up and even when I go back in my room, there is some transition between, 'Oh fuck, I don't know what I'm doing,' to, 'I am now going to write this.' And to get dressed is something to do with coming out of that inner world to the outside world and putting a face on. It's like that for me. I just have to do that.

DAVID: I heard my wife say to her mum say the other day, 'David's got his writing head on,' which basically means I'm shutting down mentally from other people.

SUZANNE: It's taken years and years and years for my friends to know that they can't just pop round for a cup of tea, because I really don't want to stop to talk to them. And people think I'm withdrawn, whatever, depressed. I come from a working-class family and all that and my mum used to say, 'Are you still depressed?' Reading was a sign of depression, and typing – that's what I did, that's what my job was to my family, typing…. All my typing had made me even more depressed according to them.

DAVID: It made you depressed and even worse.

SUZANNE: It did, it made it really bad. They could not get themselves out of that... They couldn't go and read anything cos that would be like a threat, a challenge to their worldview. My mum used to say to the neighbour, 'She's still typing and she's still against everything.'

DAVID: That would be a great title for a memoir. *Still Typing and Still Against Everything.*

SUZANNE: There's a huge truth in it. Some of my ability to tell stories comes from my mum but stories were told rather than written. That kind of thing where you go off and do something on your own is associated with depression or weird people. I read so much as a kid because I was bloody fed up with my mum, that intense reading that children do sometimes when they are quite miserable – that bit is true, but when I got away from them and did my 'typing', it wasn't depressing.

My good friends and people close to me know there's no point in them trying to give me ideas, because every idea they give me I just say, 'No that won't work.' I can see that it's really difficult for other people, because you're in your head and you're physically there but you're not really. My kids are quite good with it. I think it is really difficult to live with. So you don't want to talk to anyone and I also don't want to have anyone contradict anything that I say because that is what I'm saying.

DAVID: The contradiction thing applies to all writers. If I've got an idea for a comedy thing and somebody says that it won't work, I get very angry – 'No! It does work!'

SUZANNE: It's weird isn't it? You pretend that you really want other people's opinions... It's probably horrible for my friends, but when an editor tells me that something is not a good idea, I occasionally will pull rank: it's a good idea because I say it's a good idea. And more recently I had it with a young guy – they're all young guys, to be honest, I only have to say the word 'menopausal' and they go, 'Ewwww!' – Anyway, they were having ideas for me and it was the week that the vaccine for meningitis was in the news. My third child nearly died of meningitis, so I have quite strong feelings and knowledge about that subject, and the young guy said it wasn't a good idea. Well, I just wrote the column and sent it in… I was really annoyed because I knew it was a good idea, because I knew I had the emotional stuff and I knew the research, because my daughter had been involved in the trials.

It was a good column. Not all of the things that I write are good and I'm not proud of all of them, but that was good. And the idea that he would say that it wasn't an idea and I should do some sort of celebrity thing that week really annoyed me. But it happens.

On the other hand, when I was young, people used to say, 'Just write it', and I'd say, 'What length?' and they'd say, 'Oh, just let it roll.' I used to think, 'My God, what does that mean?' Total panic. I now see that they were trusting me but at the time I was freaked out completely – what the hell does that mean? Let it roll? I think that's one of the worst things an editor could say to me.

DAVID: Like saying, 'Do what you want.'

SUZANNE: Or, 'Write about what you did on your holidays.' Like somebody emailed me today and said, 'You've been to some festivals' – because I have, ridiculously, this year been to some festivals and I'm never ever going to do it again – 'So would you like to write a column?' I said, 'So is the line, 'I have been to some festivals?", and they said, 'Yeah.' See, that is not an idea.

DAVID: If you did write a column that involved festivals, what might it be about?

SUZANNE: 'I have been to festivals' does not seem to me to be an idea. An idea would be – I'm trying to work it out – the only thing that I would possibly write about is the work of it, how festivals are really hard work, that might be a way in for me. The idea that festivals are some sort of leisure activity when there's, oh my God, millions of things on all the time, I find really overwhelming. I took my oldest daughter to one and she had a programme and we had to go and see Hanif Kureishi speak, and then a band, and then poetry, and then some comedy – it was just non-stop. And I thought: in my actual life, my normal life, I wouldn't go to an exhibition and a talk and all these things in one day. I can't remember hardly any of it, it all just goes into a blur… And then the other bit of course is just being young and dancing and taking drugs, which you don't need to be at a festival to do.

Yeah, an idea is when the thing you bring to it will make it slightly different to everyone else's idea. Not much different, just slightly different. But I know that that column – 'I have been to some festivals' – will be written, but I don't want to do it.

DAVID: Is it hard for you to turn down a column?

SUZANNE: There is that freelance mentality where you're offered work and you feel that you should take it. I still feel like that.

DAVID: It's a hindrance in a way. You know that you must turn things down, but it's a compulsion to take any and all kinds of work. If somebody said to me, 'Will you write a million words for *Gardening Today* for ten pence?' I'll do it.

SUZANNE: I'm good on the money thing now. Last time, I didn't tell *The Telegraph* that I wouldn't do a piece because I didn't have the time, I told them that they weren't paying me enough.

DAVID: For a lot of writers, talking about money, negotiating contracts, and anything to getting paid what you think the job is worth is very difficult. Do you have any advice on financial matters?

SUZANNE: Whatever they offer, get them to double it. They always have a bit more. It's kind of crap and I don't think money is the only thing about it, but I increasingly resent being asked to write for free. I might have made this up but the High Commission of (nation deleted) asked me to do a talk. I said, 'What is the fee?' and they said, 'There isn't one.' To stand up and talk in front of respected people is a lot of work, so what do you mean there's no fee?

I really resent that everyone is being asked to work for free. I used to write columns where they'd offer me £250 and I'd say, 'Double it and give half of it to a domestic violence charity', if the piece was on domestic violence, and they could do it because they had those budgets. That was fine, I was quite happy to do that but everyone at the moment is just being asked to do it for nothing.

DAVID: Young writers coming up will take it as a given.

SUZANNE: They are. I've lately had some younger writers send me really heart-breaking emails, because they think I've done OK and I can tell them what to do. It's hard. If any of my kids said that they want to do this, I would say, 'You need some other skill now as well.' A bit like it used to be with acting or something.

And we finish our crustaceans and leave, off into a harsher world than the one we started working in. The idea that somehow you've fallen into a world where the job you're best at is one you might not get paid to do is a terrifying one. But even when you do get paid, you find yourself having jumped from out of the working-for-nothing frying pan and into a fire made of – tax! Invoices! Late payers! And a lot of other frightening things that only a superhero or an accountant can help you with.

Our next interviewee is both of those things.

CHAPTER FOUR

CATHERINE ROSENTHAL
– 'Lovely Interesting People Who Are Great To Work With'

In the increasingly vague structure of this book, I am now nearing a point in my writer's day where it's lunchtime for our fictitious writer. (N.B I could have said 'scribe' there, if I wanted to do the thing of not repeating a word I've just used. But as 'scribe' is a word as loathsome as 'penning' for 'writing' I have decided to say 'writer'. You've got to have standards. Anyway.)

Lunchtime for a writer, fictitious or otherwise, is great. Because first of all, it's lunchtime and that means something to eat and drink. Also you get to stop working. And sometimes you get to feel like you're slightly important and you go and have lunch with someone who wants to talk about you. Like your agent. Or your accountant.

I have a mild bee in my bonnet about accountants. Like the names Colin and Barry, accountants were the default target for comedians without imagination for most of my childhood (it may or may not have helped that my dad, who is far from dull, was an accountant). It's especially annoying that this slur was propagated by people who, without boring old accountants to regulate their finances, would be begging for pennies on a sea front. (And so I always feel sympathetic for those rogue accountants who, presumably tiring of the 'accountants are boring' jokes, embezzle their clients' money. I would.)

Writers need accountants for the same reasons that most self-employed people need accountants or any other professionals: to do work for them that they are ill-equipped to do themselves. With the irregularity of a writer's work, the unpredictability of revenue streams and the much-feared shadow of the 'spike' (a one-off surge in income which can suddenly, horrifyingly engorge your tax bill), it makes a great deal of sense to not only engage an accountant but treat them with the respect and fear with which you would a doctor or a plumber.

There's also the added factor that, unlike many other self-employed people who seem to have no problem sending invoices, collecting receipts or generally maintaining routine paperwork, writers are thrown daily into hysterical panic at the thought of anything to do with money and will spend most of their free time emailing their accountants in tears at the merest hint of a letter from the Inland Revenue. If agents are like surrogate parents to writers, telling them that they're great and everyone else is silly, then accountants are like nannies, reassuring them that everything's going to be all right and the taxman is silly.

For these and many other reasons, I have (and you should have) great respect for accountants, who have to put up a lot from their sobbing clients. And I am extremely lucky to have as my accountant Catherine Rosenthal, who has never been boring in her life.

I went out for lunch with Catherine to a restaurant near her office and, after a general chat about the fact that writers can be 'needy', we moved on to the central theme of the relationship between writers and accountants: money.

DAVID: A lot of writers when they start have no idea about money. Would you say that writers are famously bad with money?

CATHERINE: I think on average that's not an unreasonable thing to say but there are some very strong exceptions to the rule. You do get some people who are very, very good with money, notwithstanding the fact that you'd imagine them to be terribly scatter-brained. But I think as a general point to make about writing, it's a fair generalization.

DAVID: When I started out in my twenties, I was extremely lucky to have my dad to offer me advice – although for the record, he would like me to point out that he is a certified accountant and not a chartered accountant.

CATHERINE: Did he help you?

DAVID: The first thing he said to me was, 'Do your tax', and it's amazing how many twenty-year-old music journalists, people who in those days were signing on at the same time, weren't sure what their liability was. An awful lot of my friends in their late twenties would say to me, 'How do you do your finances?' I used to do my own at first because I was only earning a small amount of money at the time so I was able to do my own tax. What percentage of your clients are writers?

CATHERINE: About a third – it could be more than that. I've probably dealt with, over the years, up to 100. It's difficult to say. Most of them tend to stay as clients. Maybe it's inertia, or maybe they're just very happy with me. I hope it's because they're very happy with me. Some clients come and go but I've had many of them for a long time.

DAVID: Do you find writers lean on you? Sometimes I think that writers act like children when it comes to accountants, always crying, 'Help me! Help me!'

CATHERINE: Yes, I think there is an element of that, but I wouldn't want to say that nobody else is like that, so don't think that you're completely on your own. It's not just writers. It could be anyone. I'm dealing with someone at the moment who's a bit like that and he's not a writer. There is a certain element of having to go back to absolute basics and help people. And that's fine, that's what we're there for, so I don't have a problem with that. Accountants are in the business of helping people to get their affairs right and helping them to manage to live within their means. The most important thing is to do the compliance, make sure you don't get into trouble with the Inland Revenue. That's probably what people see us as most important for. But it can be a bit more basic than that, with an accountant saying to someone, 'OK, this is how much you have to live on, this is how much you've got to spend and this is how you can live within your means.'

DAVID: Writers are self-employed and that situation brings with it fear and insecurity and instability. Is this something you find you have to deal with on a regular basis?

CATHERINE: Absolutely. It's very stressful being self-employed. Don't get me wrong, there are many benefits for a lot of people. A lot of people hate being employed and they hate having to work for someone and being told what to do, and being self-employed can be lovely in many ways. You can work in your bedclothes all day. I know a number of writers who became writers because they didn't want to get dressed in the morning. It does give you a lot of freedom, but it does give you anxiety as well because there's no regular money coming in a lot of the time. You don't know where it's coming from so you've got to be awfully careful managing your finances, not putting your head in the sand, and recognizing problems.

DAVID: If you're someone who doesn't like to be employed, then by definition you're someone who doesn't like stability and order. People who are employed are better at budgeting and will say things like, 'I can't come out tonight because I can't afford to.' Whereas if you're self-employed, you might ignore that fact and say, 'Yeah, why not?'

CATHERINE: Exactly. You might say, 'I've got lots of money in my account' when really you should be thinking, 'Oh dear, I forgot that's for my VAT, that's for the tax I've got to pay in three months' time.' And really some of the money that seems to be available for me to spend is money I should be saving, because I'm not going to get another cheque in for three months, so it's my next three months' budget I'm spending.

DAVID: There is that cliché of famine and feast.

CATHERINE: Definitely. And I think again that's the problem with writers, particularly if you're a novelist. Maybe less these days because the advances are smaller, but if you've got a really fantastic advance, you've now got to finish the book. You might be writing it from scratch, depending on whether it's your first novel or not, you might have already presented a draft, but you'll be getting a lovely advance. But that could be meant to last you for two or three years, depending on how fast a writer you are.

DAVID: Or you can take the hack approach. 'I've got an £50,000 advance. If I write this book in a year, that advance gives me £950 a week. If I take five years to write it, that advance only gives me £190 pounds a week…'

CATHERINE: I do have one client who'd written a novel beforehand and it was successful, and then he started writing this second book that took him the best part of fourteen years to write. It seems mad, and what's weird is that now he's become quite prolific and has started bashing out a book every couple of years, but that second book was a major problem. And he had to go back and live at home with his parents and not earn any money for fourteen years, just working in his bedroom at home.

DAVID: You can't rely on yourself as a writer. You can't even say, 'Right, in two years' time, I'll have finished this book', because you don't know if you will or not.

CATHERINE: That's absolutely correct. It can be pretty unpredictable is the best way to put it. I think in this particular case, he didn't care about material things, he just was compelled to finish this book. He's just a complete artist. I think it's amazing. I couldn't do it.

DAVID: Do you have clients with the opposite of that attitude? I'm a bit of a hack in a lot of ways, always getting little jobs while looking for big ones, essentially just grabbing at things. Is that fairly common?

CATHERINE: Yes, particularly among people who've done journalism. It's tricky in the journalistic world these days, isn't it? Really, really hard. I've had people who've been journalists and then moved maybe into other things as well, or maybe done a bit of both because the journalism has definitely died down. They definitely do take anything going because they don't want to feel they haven't got enough to live on. I completely understand that, I'd probably be like that if I was capable of writing. The problem with journalism is that it's so difficult to get well-paid journalistic work. I'm not sure there's enough out there to sustain people generally. There are a few well-known journalists who've got some good paid gigs with their newspapers or have regular writing jobs, but there just seems to be very little to go around at the moment.

DAVID: It does seem that a lot of people are working for free now.

CATHERINE: It's the internet, isn't it? Everyone wants to read things for free, people are blogging for nothing, people are following blogs, and people see the internet as a free resource that doesn't cost them anything. But actually there is a cost, it's just not being picked up directly by the end consumer. People are doing work for free to get publicity. There's also the cost of running websites; the newspapers mainly have websites and most of them don't charge for their content. They obviously just see it as something they have to do, so in those cases newspapers are picking up the tab. As far as I understand many of them are not making profits. There is the advertising income, but in terms of news many newspapers are not making good profits and some of them are making losses on a regular basis. It's a difficult model. I'm not going to claim to be an expert on it, but people are really used to getting things for free now, they don't want to pay.

DAVID: You're living in a world where you can have a million hits on YouTube and no income and you just hope that

that leads to something, selling some advertising space or getting a record deal… How long have you been doing this job?

CATHERINE: I've been doing this job for over twenty years.

DAVID: Have you noticed any change in the way that people are paid, in terms of earning patterns?

CATHERINE: I think that with novelists, there are some changes in the patterns. There was a period when the advances got quite high and there was this debate about would you rather have big advances or would you rather have the royalties afterwards? And there was a period when advances got very high and people wouldn't earn them out. The advances are much lower these days. I think the publishers are running scared and the advances are going down so even quite established writers who were hoping for good advances aren't getting them. And very established writers want a big advance on their next novel and it's a real battle, the publishers don't want to pay these giant advances and risk making a loss on them. It's an interesting one. Advances peaked before the recession. They were offering silly amounts for some debut novels, unbelievable amounts of money. Don't get me wrong, it's a precarious profession, I'm not going to pretend that it was an easy area to make money in, but certainly publishers take much less chance on these things now.

I think generally advances have gone down a lot, but I guess there's still a chance to earn on the royalties if you can get your book out there and it's a big seller. There are so many people fighting now. With the internet you can self-publish, and there's so much noise. How do you get your book out there? That's the issue. It's easy to do technically, hard to stand out. Again, not really my area in a way but I have had a couple of clients who have self-published successfully. Interestingly one of them, his other profession was as an internet marketer, so maybe if you've got expertise in internet marketing that may be a good way to go if you're also a writer. I can't swear the two things are connected. They may well be.

DAVID: They are in my case. I wrote an eBook which I publicized through my Twitter account (@quantick) and Facebook, and I've also written a novel called *The Mule* for Unbound, which I funded through friends and through relentless self-publicizing. It definitely helps if you have any kind of social media presence. I got that through emailing friends but also using Twitter and Facebook.

But that's enough about me. What are, in your experience, typical horror stories for writers?

CATHERINE: Some of the worst ones with writers have been to do with a demand for contracts, I've seen one or two cases where agents have agreed to do a worldwide deal on a book. So you might get the UK publisher saying, 'Well, I'll publish it but I need the world rights,' which means it's much harder to go and get better deals in other countries, and you're just hoping for the best that your UK publisher will do a good job on the worldwide rights. You've got all your eggs in one basket. I think I've seen two or three instances of that that I thought were possibly not right, and the writer was quite upset about it. But really I think bad deals for the writer occur generally when the agent just wanted an easy life. And I think that's really unfair. I know it's more effort to go and sell books in different territories but I think agents are being unethical in that situation.

DAVID: Do you find that writers tend not to stand up for themselves?

CATHERINE: It depends. They're all really different. Some are very forthright. Some can be very business-like, which isn't what you'd necessarily expect, but I have encountered writers like that from time to time. They do quite a lot of research and approach the whole business scientifically. They do a lot of leg work, they go round all the festivals. And they think they've got a formula, but they may not have, they may have just been lucky with that one book. I had one writer who had a fantastic worldwide bestseller, which did particularly well in the States, and he did a lot of turning up at book fairs all round the world, pushing the book, talking about the book to the customers, and there was a lot of word of mouth going on. But having said that, with him thinking he'd cracked it, the next book was not a great success. And he got a fantastic advance which as a result just didn't turn out. The publisher was obviously hoping the next one would do as well and it didn't hit the same vibe or whatever.

DAVID: So many things are a mystery. When I was doing interviews for *How To Write Everything*, I spoke to Ben Aaronovitch and Andrew Cartmel, both authors, and they told me that the trick is not to rip off the latest bestseller, this year's *Harry Potter* or *Fifty Shades Of Grey*, but to have the same idea at the same time as the person who's going to write this year's bestseller. It still takes a year to get a book out and you can't sit there and say that next year books about bondage and wizards are going to be the thing.

CATHERINE: You can't. Those runaway major bestsellers that you mention, nobody would have ever guessed in advance that they would have taken off. That's the fundamental unknowable, particularly about novel writing. Did you ever read a book about the financial system called *Black Swan*? A black swan is an event that's almost completely unpredictable and changes everything, like the collapse of the financial system in 2008 which no one could have really predicted in advance. And the internet can almost be seen as a black swan, with the effect it's had on publishing, on the music business, and on newspapers – it's had an absolutely devastating effect on newspaper income, and that's something that you could really not have predicted which completely changed everything. And in a way they described writing, particularly novels, books, in the sense that to have a bestseller is one of those things you could never predict. That's the thing about writing, it's just a horribly unpredictable career, particularly for book writers. You could write a beautiful book that everyone says is wonderful, or you can write a very trivial bit of rubbish and nobody knows which book will be the one that sells ten copies or a 100 million. Publishers don't know, agents don't know. They know it's a good book but that's as far as they can go.

It's really, really hard. I'm an accountant, I've got X number of clients and I charge on average X amount – everyone obviously will be charged differently depending on how much work it is – but I can predict within a reasonable degree of accuracy what my income will be next year based on the amount of time I spend and the fees that I know I will bill clients. I know within five or ten per cent what my income is likely to be next year. And I have no problem knowing that, in spite of all the uncertainties in the world, my income will be such and such. If you're a writer... in a year or two you may well know what you're going to earn because you've got agreements in place, but at the start of your career you've just got no idea what you might be going to earn. You don't know how your book's going to do, you don't know how many copies it's going to sell. It's just utterly, utterly unpredictable. So for a writer, X amount of work could produce a million pounds of income, or it could produce a thousand pounds of income, or it could produce no income.

DAVID: Would you say that being a writer is one of the most uncertain jobs?

CATHERINE: Yes, definitely. A writer, or a musician in a pop band, or something like that.

DAVID: So being a writer is as bad as being a musician...

CATHERINE: I would have thought so, pretty much. I suppose if you're a musician you can go out and get gigs, can't you? They might not be paid brilliantly but you could earn a crust if you're any good. So it's not necessarily a complete disaster. But if you're writing your own music and hoping to do well and sell it, there's just no guarantee that that will be... and it's a bit like that, being a novelist anyway. Obviously if you're a paid journalist working regularly for a newspaper it's a different matter. But we're not generally talking about that. You could be in employment, but almost all writers are self-employed.

DAVID: What sort of thing do writers have in common?

CATHERINE: Financially in common? I don't know. I'd think they all must have some urge to create something, I suppose, something generally new and different, and that's amazing. I think it's fantastic that someone can just create something out of nothing through their imagination. I'm just an accountant, but I read books too and I think, 'How could someone have thought of that from scratch?' From a financial point of view, they do tend to be a bit scattier, a bit more head in the sand than most people, a bit more worried by financial matters. I think it's a genuine concern. It's often something they don't like to think about, but it's really important that it's something that they get to grips with from the outset. And possibly people want to become writers at the worst time, so I would say don't give up your day job if you're doing something else, work at something however unbearable it may be, until you feel you've got a foothold into writing. I wouldn't necessarily just give up everything and be a novelist now unless you've got a fantastic amount of savings and you've got enough to keep you going indefinitely. I'm not saying it's easy but it's something you could do alongside another job maybe. If you really want to do it.

DAVID: It's a job that you can do anywhere and it's a job you can do for an hour a day. If you wanted to be a lumberjack, you couldn't really do it in your spare time.

CATHERINE: There's that famous thing about Anthony Trollope. He was the Postmaster-General, and he got up at five in the morning every day and wrote 1000 words or however many words before he had to go to work. A quite unbelievable amount of discipline.

DAVID: Do you find writers to be undisciplined, scruffy and drunk in their approach to things?

CATHERINE: I wouldn't say they seem scruffier than most people to be honest. I think if you're going to be a successful writer, you've got to be disciplined in the writing. Anyone who is a successful writer has to be disciplined, certainly a lot of the time, otherwise it's going to be really hard to survive if you're not. Whether that discipline always spills over to financial matters I don't know. Possibly not.

I don't think writers are scruffier or personally more disciplined, but I'm not sitting with them, watching what they're doing every day. And I don't know if they were they would necessarily tell me the truth about it.

DAVID: They are, after all, writers who've got an accountant.

CATHERINE: That's right, the fact that they've got an accountant may well mean that they want to be disciplined, and they don't want to get into trouble. There may be a whole raft of writers out there who think, 'Oh I can't afford an accountant,' who may be getting into terrible trouble. Or maybe they're very efficient and perfectly capable of dealing with it themselves, who knows?

DAVID: At what point in someone's career should they go and see an accountant?

CATHERINE: I think they should see an accountant early on irrespective. It may be that they don't need one straightaway but I think they should have a chat if they're unclear of tax rules or how things will get reported.

DAVID: What do you mean by reporting?

CATHERINE: Well, they're earning from their writing, so they need to know what their obligations are to do a tax return, when they need to tell the Inland Revenue that they've got a source of income, when the return has to be submitted, how much they need to put aside to pay their tax... I think they should do that from right at the beginning, as soon as they start earning money from it.

DAVID: Most people don't do that because they're frightened.

CATHERINE: I think you're probably right. Or they think, 'I can put it off, I can sort it out in a few months' time.' It could be that in a few months' time is too late, they've already got into a problem. Certainly if you're going to sign a contract to do some work, if you've got dribs and drabs of income, you can tell the Revenue yourself and declare that. If you're reasonably IT literate you can go online, register, maybe file a small tax return. But if you're about to sign a contract with anybody to write a book or to do a major piece of work, I think that you should speak to an accountant, ideally before you sign the contract.

DAVID: What do you see as the accountant's role? Presumably as not making vast amounts of money by tricking the taxman.

CATHERINE: Definitely not. Just from my personal point of view, I would never actively encourage people to go into tax schemes. I have to say that most writers I've dealt with have never been in the slightest bit interested in schemes they can go into to save vast amounts of tax. And generally speaking I've always viewed those schemes as being very risky one way or the other, because even though they tend to come with these counsels' opinions attached – where a counsel is saying, 'We think this is

OK because because because' – you know there's going to be a tax investigation. There will be automatically with any of these tax schemes because you have to declare them upfront. So you know you're going to be subjected to stress and I know that most writers don't want that, they don't want stress from knowing that they're subject to a tax investigation. I think an accountant's role is to try and help you comply with tax rules, to not get into trouble and to structure your affairs in a tax efficient way as is completely permitted by the rules, no more than that. Make sure they're aware of any nasties and areas where you can get into trouble, be aware generally of the VAT rules.

DAVID: From your personal point of view, what are the best and worst things about working with writers?

CATHERINE: The best things are the people, I think they're great people to work with. I think they're interesting and fun and different, I just think they're a fabulous group of people. Writers are the most interesting people to deal with just on a level of purely getting pleasure from the job. The best bit of the job is meeting clients, and writers are probably the most fun. I just think they're lovely interesting people who are great to work with. So that's the best thing. I don't have a problem with the fact that they may be quite dependent on you and quite needy of your advice, I actually like that. I'm not saying they all are dependent and needy, but I think I actually like that.

Most people who go into accountancy see it as a service industry where you want to help the client. That's what you do. I quite like the fact that they need your help and they may think they're asking silly questions but they're often not. They're usually very fundamental and important questions, however embarrassed you may feel about asking them. I think they're usually valid and important questions and it's much better to say, 'I don't know this, can I ask you this question?' than to think, 'I'm not going to ask because it will make me look silly.' Writers are the best fun to deal with and I've always felt I'm privileged to work for writers. It's something I hope I continue doing.

Worst things about writers, I can't really think of anything. I think someone coming to you with a problem after the fact can be frustrating, but to be honest that's something that happens with everyone, not just writers. I know it's very easy to say that writers are always worst at this but there are plenty of other people that come to you after the fact.

DAVID: And finally, if you could impart one piece of advice to a writer, what would it be?

CATHERINE: The key thing is always signing the contract after you've spoken to an accountant.

Lunch, then, with my accountant. I learned a lot and I enjoyed myself. I hope you did too (although you will have to imagine the lovely food. Mmm hmm).

CHAPTER FIVE

JOHN PANTON
– 'I Want To Make Big Films That Will Be Probably Be A Bit Odd'

I have known John Panton for a number of years. We work together regularly on short films for his production company Meat Bingo, scripting, coming up with ideas and stories, and producing a variety of material with an excellent crew and casts featuring brilliant British actors and comics.

John differs from most of the writers in the book in that not only does he have a family but he also has a full-time job, which makes being a creative type more than unusually difficult. But it was this full-time job which caused us to meet, at my old school in Exmouth, where John teaches Film Studies and Media Studies. I was back to do a talk to whatever a sixth form is called now and John gave me a tour of his classroom and then asked me to do a voice-over in one of his short films, Matt Vs Beast. After that, I sent him a script for a short film that I'd written years ago and nobody wanted to make. John made it and we took it from there. Now our films attract attention all over the world. John and his long-term artistic collaborator Moose Allain were commissioned by the group Elbow to make a video for one of their songs, and Meat Bingo's film *Welcome To Oxmouth* won the Radical Democracy Challenge award in Warsaw in 2014. John and I are currently working on Meat Bingo's first feature film.

The following interview was conducted by email and it is so neatly structured that I have left it untouched. I did go back to John to ask him to expand a few points, but it remains, both raw and elegant, in the form in which I first sent it to him. Just to be clear, I'm the one in the deafening capital letters, John in calmer and more thoughtful lower case.

PART ONE: DAWN

Awake, a new day beckons, an idea on the pad by the bedside, optimism, you are a writer. Now what?

WHAT GOT YOU WRITING?

A necessity, stemming from my desire to make short films. I knew I wanted to direct films, but didn't know any writers at the time. My first batch of self-penned short films were clunky lo-fi Sci-Fis – really quite awful but a brilliant training ground.

WHAT'S GOOD ABOUT WRITING?

The scripts I write (or the ideas I scribble down to pass on to others) are specifically to create films. The few that actually get made complete an irresistibly satisfying creative process – the original script to the final edit.

WHAT'S EXCITING ABOUT IT?

Problem solving. An unformed half-idea that start materialising into a potential workable idea, is mired by a series of problems. As each obstacle is overcome to create the story, it generates an addictive momentum.

WHEN YOU GET UP IN THE MORNING, WHAT DO YOU LOOK FORWARD TO?

I work full-time as a teacher – I teach to fourteen– nineteen year olds in one of the biggest schools in the UK, alongside overseeing staff who deliver a wide range of courses that have a vocational focus – so my brain is immediately anticipating the various classes awaiting me and their inherent challenges. If I can slot 'film development' into my thought processes as well, it creates another space that balances out the demands of the profession.

However, I'm lucky enough to be teaching a subject that I love, namely Film Studies. Sometimes I'll make my writing and film-making activities apparent to my students if I feel it'll be of some use and I'm very honest about my on-going learning alongside theirs. I also hope that I'm able to further their understanding and appreciation of film form by highlighting my own (hopefully) improving processes and my truly laughable early efforts. As I've increasingly learnt, to make the work and filmmaking balance achievable, it takes planning. Really boring planning. Months in advance. The idea generation takes place organically but then the scripting needs some allocated time set aside. Oh yeah – then the storyboarding, casting, the locations, the scheduling...

I'm far from perfect at this but in order to lessen the impact on work and family, I clearly avoid pinch points in the year. The lead up to the exam season, coursework deadlines, the delirious exhaustion at the end of the autumn term plus any family events. You know, birthdays and whatnot. I tend to schedule a film to be shot, then incrementally add specific days or week-long deadlines to achieve certain tasks, giving fair warning to my wife and attempting to make sure that the time I'm given to be off-radar is reciprocated and booked-in. As with most creative pursuits, the reality is that something will always crop up and put a spanner in the works – I've come to expect problems, so will need to re-negotiate on a regular basis.

The short film *Lot 13* had a schedule that was set in stone, until, alas, the original location for the shoot became unavailable. A last-minute location was found and frantic changes were made: minor to the script, but difficult to rejig storyboards and technical considerations (as it turned out, the new location was a far better fit for the script). Therefore, time needed to be set aside and negotiated.

I realize that using the word 'negotiate' sounds rather formal but as my writing and filmmaking has developed it has taken on a new mantle. From the initial *hobby*, it's now a second *job*. Even though most of what I have done up to this point is no-budget fiction film making, it's clearly work. Treating it as thus has also helped my approach, perhaps developing a growing seriousness, more graft (lots more rewrites!) and a sustained work ethic.

DOES HAVING A FAMILY MAKE YOU LESS CREATIVE OR MAKE YOU FOCUS ON THE TIME YOU HAVE TO CREATE STUFF?

I certainly didn't expect to be in a position I am now, starting to look seriously at the possibility of a low-budget feature (and currently working with Creative England and the BFI). What a daft time of my life to get really busy – I've got three kids, all boys, who seem to exhaustingly obey every 'boy' stereotype imaginable. To put it politely, they can be a bit of a handful in their unrelentingly boisterous approach to life. I'm baffled by my own stupidity – why didn't I get properly motivated before I had children?

Perhaps strangely, it's my children who've given me my motivation. Far from stifling creativity, I've found that the emotional resonances of witnessing their births (one in particular was, quite frankly, harrowing), their continual changes as they grow and the perception that time has sped up since they arrived, has accentuated an awareness of mortality. My meandering twenties morphed into a surprisingly focused thirties. There's also an extra level of confidence and life experience that they've brought that has led me to a point whereby I agree to make things that I genuinely have *no idea* how to make.

A case in point is the short film *Valentina's Dream*, which you wrote. For a no-budget production, it set some challenges i.e. it depicts Russia's iconic cosmonaut Valentina Tereshkova, it's set in Moscow and well, on *Mars*. I just said 'yes' because I loved the concept, and only then started worrying about how to make it. David sent me a bare-bones script, allowing me as ever to add whatever I felt could make it work visually. Mulling over various approaches, chatting to artists (Moose Allain and Jeremy Marshall) and visual effects people (Graham Salisbury) culminated in a live action green screen shoot with animated backgrounds and motion graphics added later. The restrictions of 'no-budget whatsoever' arguably forced a more inventive and stylized take on the original script.

PART TWO: MORNING

Behind the desk, at the office, on the kitchen table, it's time to start.

WHERE DO YOU WORK?

Anywhere. On a bus, a train, in a break at work, at home, at the swimming pool while the kids have lessons, cafes…

WHAT ARE YOUR QUIRKS?

Quirks are a luxury. I don't have time for quirks.

WHAT IS YOUR OFFICE SET UP?

I don't have a dedicated office for writing. I would like one though.

DO YOU HAVE MUSIC OR SILENCE?

If I've got longer than an hour to write without interruptions, music really helps to focus – certain pieces of music create the right mood to suit the film concept, or certain pieces are structured in a way that they maintain pace. Music with a fractured structure can sometimes keep the mind alert.

DO YOU HAVE PICTURES OR GAMES?

Even though my drawing skills are somewhat limited, I might scribble out images or odd expressionistic sketches that seem to point to a possible structure.

DO YOU HAVE A ROUTINE FOR THE MORNING?

Water. Porridge. Espresso. Get to work.

WHAT ARE YOUR INTERRUPTIONS, WELCOME OR OTHERWISE?

I have three children so I have long since accepted I will ALWAYS be interrupted. So, presuming thus, I'm more likely to make notes as I go, so I don't lose my thread. I use Celtx a lot for scriptwriting and keep adding notes to the side of the page. On the rare occasions where I think I'm on to a really good idea and I'm on child care duties after work, I might just leave the laptop on and in between cooking for/bathing/reading stories with the kids, keep typing notes as ideas occur. Admittedly, this is distracted parenting and clearly not ideal on a regular basis – but at least once notes are in place, it's then possible to book time to start formulating into script form.

PART THREE: IN TRANSIT

Having a break, getting ideas, escape from the computer.

WHAT METHODS DO YOU USE TO GENERATE IDEAS?

I have the luxury of not depending on ideas to create an income, so I let ideas rattle around and prioritize as and when I want to pursue a particular one.

WHAT DO YOU DO WHEN YOU'RE STUCK?

Jog. I run a really specific route and the familiarity allows my mind to wander. The different context, the inability to stay stuck staring at a screen and the adrenaline seems to encourage other perspectives. Added to this – you notice things. People going about their business. Who are they? Different houses. Who lives there?

Incidentally, my short film *Line Signal* sprung directly from jogging. Admittedly, my physique doesn't quite fit the jogger mould (my Hitchcock-esque cameo right at the end of Elbow's *Lost Worker Bee* video evidences my only similarity with the master might be my waistline) but as a mental cleanser it offers a de-stress from the work environment, time to ruminate problems and a springboard for new ideas. My route takes me along a deserted rail track, with one particularly poignant location reflecting the Beeching Cuts – the underside of a bridge, overgrown and blocked by a mound of earth. I will confess I always jogged a little bit faster in that spot, as it was the furthest point from any housing and well, a bit spooky.

Every time I ran past, I couldn't help but see it in an increasingly cinematic light. Something started forming. Spookiness + Beeching Cuts + the desire to try a new genre = lots of research into Beeching himself, how the local area was affected, investigation into local ghost stories. Piece by piece a clear idea eventually formed. Lots of versions of the script were produced, with the very welcome input of a script editor to keep things on track (pun intended).

WHAT DO YOU DO FOR A BREAK?

Due to my lifestyle, writing is a break. Adding film making to the demands of my job isn't easy. But let's face it – the teaching profession isn't the happiest profession. In fact, do I know a really 'happy' teacher? I teach at a great school, but the ongoing cycle of governments changing concept of what education actually *is*, means that the profession is under considerable pressure to evidence and support whichever current educational mindset is in vogue. The focus on statistics, instead of the individual nature of the students (and the often uncontrollable external effects from their lives outside of school) creates a job preoccupied with percentages. One of the reasons I started making short films was I could see the love for my subject ebbing away. It was a way to regain enthusiasm, and in turn, hopefully pass on that positive enthusiasm to the students.

Separately to this and for my sense of self – it allows me to have a break from governmental tide turning and actually make stuff. There's only so many times you can draw a box with a face inside it on a whiteboard and say, 'This is a close-up'. I'd rather make a film and then use it as an example – 'I did this because' …

IS THERE SUCH A THING AS WRITER'S BLOCK?
Yes. Get some exercise away from a computer.

WHAT KEEPS YOU AT THE COMPUTER?
If time allows, the enjoyment of increased writing speed as the ideas start to coalesce.

DO YOU CARRY A NOTEPAD AND ALL THAT?
I often have a notebook and will type random notes into my phone if an idea strikes.

PART FOUR: PANIC
No work, no phone calls, now what?

HOW DO YOU GET WORK – YOU OR AGENT?
Me.

WHAT IS AN AGENT FOR?
I don't know. Do I need one?

HOW DO YOU GENERATE WORK?
My work is mostly self-generated.

HOW DO YOU SELL YOUR IDEAS?

Stemming from my self-generated film projects, I've now started to accept enquiries from people approaching me for commercial work. Through the course of making a series of short films over the last five years or so, I've unintentionally created a portfolio of work that now functions as a way of saying, 'I can make stuff like this.' Luckily people have liked my work and supported me to the point that now I've been offered paid work.

Through the democratic joy of Twitter (I know it gets a bad press but just follow nice people and block any aggressive types) the keyboardist and producer for Elbow, Craig Potter, supported an early film, *Falcon of Fury* and the following releases, either retweeting or saying nice things about the subsequent films. He's also a big fan of consummate Twitter user and artist Moose Allain, who I've been lucky to work with on a few film projects. He approached Moose, and in turn, me, asking about the possibility of a music video. Moose was to provide the story and I would direct.

I said no. I didn't want to turn it down, but I had to. Too busy at school, and because I'm a control freak, the deadline was horribly close and the filming approach suggested didn't quite fit with what I'm interested in. I was of course deeply worried I'd made an AWFUL decision. However, a month or so went by and the band came calling again...

A production company was going to take on the project but couldn't schedule it. But this time, I had the time. I was able to take the story from Moose, script it, storyboard it, schedule it and along with the help of the amazing people who've worked with me in the past, produced a video in record time that thankfully met with the approval of Universal. It was a scary learning curve, especially being flung into the requirements of a demanding contract, but an experience that hopefully readies me for any future contracts.

WHERE DO YOU GO?

I don't.

IS IT WHO YOU KNOW OR WHAT YOU KNOW?

Both. People in the industry have seemed to have liked my work. Word has spread through Twitter and I've been supported and promoted by those professionals. *Lot 13* is an example of this – stand-up and writer Simon Evans agreed to star which I duly announced on Twitter. One of my favourite Twitter users, Sanjeev Kohli, responded, cheekily asking for a part (yes!). This interest expanded on the release of the film online, with comedians like Frankie Boyle tweeting the link to the film.

My feeling is that it's not how many views you get online, it's who sees the film. I certainly can't compete with YouTube cat videos. The following shoot was *Valentina's Dream*, for which we were honoured to have Rebecca Front starring. She saw *Lot 13* online and this helped her trust that we vaguely knew what we were up to. The traditional route for short films is the festival circuit first, hiding your work away until festival success (or lack of) has been clarified. From experience, I've deliberately chosen not to hide the films, but shout about them via Twitter for a limited time and see how they are received.

PART FIVE: LUNCH

A long lunch with media chums, feeding the kids or a sandwich at your desk?

IT'S LUNCHTIME – WHAT ARE YOU DOING?

I wander around the school site, making sure that the students aren't killing each other.

DO YOU SPEND THIS TIME WITH FAMILY, DO YOU LIKE LONG LUNCHES OR DO YOU EAT A SANDWICH AT YOUR DESK?

If it's the weekend, I'm with my family. If anyone wants to take me out for long lunches, that would also be great.

ARE YOU A CAN'T STOP I'M ON A ROLL PERSON OR A LONG-DISTANCE RUNNER PACE YOURSELF PERSON?

I can only write at random times. There's no way I can have a routine – writing has to happen around the chaos of my life. However, the 'I'm on a roll', when it happens, is an ace feeling.

PART SIX: MAKING A LIVING

Paying the bills, avoiding the poorhouse, calling the accountant.

HOW DO YOU DEAL WITH YOUR FINANCES?

This is a new area for me, having recently accepted a high profile directing job for a promo.

DO YOU LIVE IN FEAR OF PENURY AND DEBT?

I'm lucky – I have a good teaching job. For the moment at least.

DOES DEALING WITH MONEY TERRIFY YOU OR ARE YOU GOOD AT IT?

As a potential freelance/ltd company future beckons, it currently terrifies me as it's so far removed from my institutionalized security of a regular monthly pay packet. The fact that I have all those horribly dull adult financial concerns, such as a mortgage payments, monthly bills and school shoes for children (screw you Start-Rite) means I don't know yet where my 'risk worth taking' tipping point is. I have a good job and I work with some amazing people, but the thought (and the increased possibility) of making films on a bigger scale has an undeniably powerful draw. How much paid work would I need lined up to make a new career viable? Should I even contemplate it? I can't see my children benefitting from precarious financial insecurities, wreaked on them by a father selfishly pursuing an unattainable filmmaking dream...

KNOWING WHAT YOU KNOW NOW, HOW WOULD YOU ADVISE A NEWCOMER TO PROCEEED FINANCIALLY?

If you've got dependents: have a nine to five job and write around it. A job doesn't mean you can't be creative – I'm keenly aware that characters, themes and ideas emerge from the workplace, albeit reconfigured, repurposed and the context changed.

Build up a portfolio of work, paid or unpaid. Use Twitter (and Facebook if you must) and point people towards your work whilst supporting and celebrating other writers and work/TV/film/art you admire.

I'm not capable of having a daily routine that I can adhere to (I know people who militarily stick to two hours of writing per day before going to work) so even though I need time to write/plan/shoot/edit, it comes in swathes, blocks of time rather than say, an hour a day. There are periods of time where I have a normal life and I'll be back from work in time to get the kids in bed while my wife is working.

Or, for example, if I'm editing a film, I'll come back from work, hopelessly try to get the kids in bed by a sensible time, and then edit for as long as I can before tiredness wins out. Likewise, there are occasions when writing a rough script has to happen there and then, so bundling the kids to bed and then typing frantically while the ideas keep propelling you forward. I do have the flexibility of longer holidays and I try to alleviate my guilt of uneven parenting styles during term time by spending lots of time with them during the hols being active, daft and hopefully fun.

PART SEVEN: BASKING IN THE GLORY

Reviews, publication, recording, first nights, Twitter, press and publicity.

WHAT IS YOUR PERSONAL DEFINITION OF SUCCESS?

As a film maker, mainly working without a budget – how many people watch and share my films online.

WHAT IS YOUR PERSONAL DEFINITION OF FAILURE?

How few people watch my films online.

HOW DO YOU KNOW YOU'VE DONE SOMETHING GOOD?

Gut feeling, plus the reactions from people I trust.

ARE YOU A PERFECTIONIST OR A 'THAT'LL DO' KIND OF PERSON?

If I had the budgets I want, I'd be a perfectionist. However, a short film script is small enough to be nailed.

WHAT IS HIGH PRAISE TO YOU?

Someone unknown liking a short film and then trawling through previous efforts, commenting favourably.

WHAT IS A DAMNING CRITICISM TO YOU?

No one responding to a new film.

DO YOU LIKE CRITICS?

If they're bright and well informed, why not? They've got a key job to sift through the staggering myriad of new cultural works and we need decent filters. If they appreciate your work too, that's ideal.

DO YOU VALUE THE OPINIONS OF FRIENDS AND FAMILY?

They provide brutally honest viewpoints – however upsetting, they are often spot-on. My wife is the best.

DO YOU LIKE EDITORS OF ANY KIND?

Yes – I don't often have the time to truly polish a script or I can simply lose objectivity. A good editor can kick the thing into shape and give you pointers for revisions.

TO WHAT EXTENT DOES COLLABORATION COME INTO PLAY IN YOUR WORK?

Film-making demands collaboration, but it only truly works when you're matched with the right sort of folks. I've luckily had a lot of freedom with the scripts I've filmed. I've retained the core of the scripts, but added my dense visual motifs and rejigged according the reality of the shooting locations and lack of budget.

DO YOU LIKE DIRECTORS?

They're obsessive control freaks with a complete lack of regard for the writing process.

PART EIGHT: RELAXING

Time out from the job or a busman's holiday?

IS WRITING LITERALLY YOUR LIFE?

No. Film making is heading that way but I would love to write more and develop my confidence. I simply don't have long enough stretches of time to devote to it.

IS IT YOUR LIVELIHOOD OR MORE THAN YOUR LIVELIHOOD?

I'm at an odd stage, where film-making (and therefore writing/developing scripts) is becoming a bigger deal. I can't foresee the final outcome but a film making livelihood wouldn't be sniffed at.

HOW DO YOU DEAL WITH FREE TIME?

I try to get more film projects developed.

DO YOU PARTITION OFF WORK AND THE REST OF YOUR LIFE?

I'm not great at this. I sometimes cross the line where a film project is so utterly consuming it negatively affects the people I love the most. I turn into a stressed uncommunicative berk until a film has finished shooting. My wife and kids miss out, sometimes when I'm in the same room as them – my filmy headspace restricts the attention they deserve.

DO YOU HAVE HOLIDAYS?

Yes, but alongside childcare I do try to make films during them. Or write.

DO OTHERS HAVE DEMANDS ON YOUR TIME? IF SO DO YOU WELCOME THESE DEMANDS?

My wife is extraordinarily supportive and I wouldn't be able to make films if it wasn't for her ability to scoop up the children and parent them in a wonderfully creative context, while I selfishly disappear for film shoots and meetings. Bearing in mind she is also a tutor and a school governor, she is an incredible ally. My three kids (like all young kids) are DEMANDING. But amazing.

WHAT IS FUN FOR YOU?

Getting a film script into production.

WHAT IS HELL FOR YOU?

When I get the family/film balance wrong. When the shoot goes badly.

PART NINE: FINISHING

Writing 'The End' or grabbing at the document as the courier comes to take it.

DOES A PIECE OF WORK EVER REALLY END? IF SO WHEN?

Yes. Even though there's aspects you'll never be happy with, once a film has been edited and released, it's good to put it behind you. George Lucas could learn a thing or two from me.

DO YOU HAVE ANY FINISHING RITUALS?

Once the film is released, go to the pub.

DO YOU WANT TO GRAB THE WORK BACK FROM THE PERSON MAKING IT PUBLIC?

I've been lucky enough to control all my releases until now. I'll have to wait and see.

PART TEN: THE WEE WEE HOURS – DOUBT, FEAR AND INSOMNIA

Why am I doing this? What's the point? I'm going to starve aren't I? And then the sun rises on a new day.

WHAT MAKES YOU DOUBT WHAT YOU DO?

It's mood related. I'm either in a confident mood or I'm feeling insecure. There's no real pattern. Time of day. Tiredness.

WHAT MAKES YOU THINK YOU MIGHT BE GOOD?

Bearing in mind I've no industry background and I'm a full-time teacher, I'm being supported and enabled by industry types, which gives me hope. Plus, I wouldn't get anything done if I was too plagued by self-doubt. I like what I do. If it's not particularly successful, learn from it and make the next one better.

HOW, IF AT ALL, WOULD YOU JUSTIFY YOUR LIFE AS A WRITER TO SOME SORT OF WEIRD SUPERNATURAL COURT?

I would be currently unable to justify my life as a writer. Director – yes.

WHAT ARE WRITERS FOR?

Enabling cool stuff to get made.

AND FINALLY – WHAT DO YOU WANT FROM THE FUTURE? SPECIFICALLY AND GENERALLY?

I WANT TO MAKE BIG FILMS THAT WILL BE PROBABLY BE A BIT ODD.

Bold and capitals John's own. Admirable decisiveness!

CHAPTER SIX

JO UNWIN
– 'I Read Through
Endless, Endless, Endless Crap'

I have known Jo Unwin in various capacities for many years. I first came across her on the television, as a brilliant comic actress. Then I would see her from time to time in meeting rooms in her capacity as a comedy writer. And more recently I've run into her in her latest and greatest incarnation as a literary agent, a job to which she is suited like a little hood is suited to a falcon.

Literary agents, like all agents, have to guide writers through their careers but they have the added task of guiding those writers through every stage of the process, from telling them what they think of a manuscript to seeing a book into print. It's a complex and detail-heavy job and requires massive reserves of brain power, charm and determination. Which is probably why Jo is so good at it. These days she represents a very large amount of writers, from Jesse Armstrong and Charlie Brooker to Georgia Pritchett and Jenny Colgan, all of whom are great.

After meeting in her very small, very book-lined office, we went down the Portobello Road to a Japanese canteen and had all kinds of stuff for lunch. (I didn't do all these interviews in one week, by the way. I'd be the size of a house if I did. Well, the size of a larger house, anyway.)

DAVID: Lunch with an agent is one of the big clichés associated with being a writer. Is lunching part of your life with writers?

JO: I go out to lunch a lot, but it's more often with publishers and editors. The classic boozy lunch where an agent goes out with a publisher which previously I thought was a complete farce is really useful, because you're being a matchmaker and you're matchmaking writers with editors. Through all the gossiping, you find out what they need. In terms of my clients, I go out with them for lunch maybe once or twice a year, but lunch isn't a big thing for me with my clients.

DAVID: Why is that? Do you have much face time with clients?

JO: Yes I do. I go out for drinks with them on an evening, but I think lunches are more celebratory, beyond the day to day talking and business of being an agent with them. When I have proper meetings with them, I'm either doing it on the phone or face to face in my office or over tea.

DAVID: How many clients have you got and have I heard of any of them?

JO: I have got apparently about twenty – you've heard of Charlie Brooker and Richard Ayoade … Jenny Colgan, she's very friendly and she's very funny on Twitter. My clients tend to have something a bit funny about them, they tend to have some warped sense of humour about them and I definitely feel that some of them are becoming really good friends.

DAVID: Do you feel that you come from a similar background to your writers? You've been a comic actress and a comedy writer. Do you feel kinship with them or is it just coincidence?

JO: I think when I first started out it helped that I knew what it was like to be edited, what it was like to be rejected and what it was like to have people lord it over your work. So I probably do have a bit of understanding about what that feels like. But I quite like reading books that are set in worlds I have no connection with at all.

DAVID: You're not just a comedy agent?

JO: No, definitely not. Comedy's a tiny part and I'm just doing my first memoir.

DAVID: And what exactly is it that you do?

JO: I help people. I help people in their writing careers. But in the first instance I spot talent out of an unbelievably huge slush pile, as it's called, and read through endless, endless, endless crap. Very often in a collection of thirty manuscripts, there'll be absolutely nothing.

DAVID: Where does this come from?

JO: This comes from people going, 'Oh, I want an agent and I've been looking in the back of books to see who represents who…' Seeing who represents their favourite authors or going online and finding out about different agents and stuff. So they then write to me with – what I would ask for is – the first three chapters of their book. There's a lot that's really bad, that's just people who have thought, 'I haven't got a job so I'll just have a go at writing a book,' and they don't have the writerly mind-set. You spot it when someone writes every day or writes because they have to write. So those ones kind of come up to the top. There's an awful lot of people who aren't much good and you're just trying to spot the great ones.

DAVID: That's the first step. What next?

JO: Then I do lot of editing with people to get their books to be as good as they can possibly be before I send them out to editors. Once you've established an author with their publishing house, you're trying to steer them and keep them getting better and better and better, rather than jumping from house to house and book to book. So that involves really reliable good relationships with not just the editor but the whole team at the publishing house. They all understand what the author is trying to do so they're all trying to promote you in the same way and through the same channels, so that it all makes sense.

DAVID: So strategy is a big part of what you do?

JO: Definitely. Trying to make an author have a career that's notable.

DAVID: Are you familiar with the million word rule? You're supposed to write a million words before you'll ever be any good.

JO: No, but I've heard of the 10,000 hours of piano practice so I suppose it's the same. A million words, wow. A novel can be 100,000 words, so that's ten novels before you're any good. I don't know about that. I think it's pretty common that the first book an author gets published is their third. That's pretty standard. There's also an average number of drafts between it arriving on my desk and it being published, which is eight, and it's normally a third or fourth draft that comes to me. It's a hellish long game.

DAVID: So you've found a good three chapters, what happens next?

JO: I look at the synopsis and make sure that they've not just written the first three good chapters but that they've actually got a story. I ask them to send me a synopsis because then I can see that the novel has a beginning, a middle and an end, that they've sent me a complete piece of work. At that point if I'm still excited, I'll phone them and say, 'Do you want to meet up?' Sometimes I'll travel to see them, sometimes they'll come to London, sometimes they are already in London and sometimes I can't meet them but I talk on Skype or whatever. One of the things I'm checking out at that stage is if they're someone I want to work with, because you're on the phone to them at least once a week so it needs to be someone you can connect with at some immediate level.

DAVID: Have there ever been people where you thought, 'I like the writing but I don't want to ever speak to you again'?

JO: Once.

DAVID: So for the record, once because they were vile. Generally, though, are people delighted when you turn up?

JO: No, they're very nervous and excited and quite often they're dressed up. They are very excited because they think this is their dream come true, but of course it's an awfully long way between that moment and actually being published. And there are so many books published and they sink without trace. So many books that just nobody ever hears about. It's just miserable.

DAVID: So you've met them, you like them…

JO: What I do at that stage is say that I can't formally take you on until we've done a bit of work because some writers – and again this has happened maybe only twice – but some writers, you send them some editorial notes and they send it back the following day saying, 'Yep. Fixed all those, done.' And they haven't internalized the problem, they haven't really thought about what you were saying, they've just gone, 'OK yeah, change change change change tick tick tick done.' And you go back to them and say, 'No, the issues I had may have required more than that.' Some authors find it really hard to understand or connect with editorial notes, so I check them out before I properly sign them. In fact I don't really sign them until the moment that I'm sending them out to publishers.

But at that point, I tend to ask them what their dreams are, what they fantasize about. If they say, 'All I've ever wanted is to be in Penguin Modern Classics,' or 'My dream is to be published by Faber,' then I might just send it to Faber or Penguin. I also do quite a lot of work with them about what it is they've written. If it's a novel, where it's going to sit on the shelf, is it going to be commercial? Obviously we want it to have commercial legs but is it a commercial book or is it a literary book? Literary fiction has a really different way of being sold than genre fiction or commercial fiction. So I'll talk to them about what they think they've done and also what they're going to do next. Because if they're writing a children's book today and erotica tomorrow, you need to think about how you're going to position them. Nobody wants to just publish a single book. It costs a lot of money and a lot of time and strategy to work out how you're going to position a book and how you're going to get attention for it.

So they want to know that they're getting not just a book but an author and they want to know what the author's going to do next. And if the author says a children's book, age seven to ten, and the next book is a crime thriller, it's difficult for them to see how they're going to brand you or set you up as an author. So I try and understand how they think they see themselves. Sometimes that takes a bit of chatting and adjustment because some people think they're more kind of literary than they are, or they're writing for a different kind of market than I presume them to be.

DAVID: Do you get people thinking that they're literary writers when they're actually commercial writers? Or vice versa?

JO: Yes though I wouldn't say 'just' commercial, because I think commercial writing is just as impressive and just as hard, just a different style. But yeah, you get people who don't necessarily know what they've done.

DAVID: There's a massive perception that anybody can write a crime novel or a romantic novel.

JO: Wrong, wrong, wrong, wrong, wrong. I think they're really hard.

DAVID: Why?

JO: Crime needs to be really believable, really pacy, you have to really care about the characters. It's always about the character, that's always the starting point. If the characters don't come to life, the story doesn't come to life. Creating a believable character that takes you through the twists and turns of a crime novel, or that you give a shit about in a romantic novel is really, really, really, hard. I have real admiration for proper crime writers or proper romantic comedy writers.

DAVID: So where are we now in your relationship with your new writer?

JO: So now I've introduced them to a few editors and if the editors like their work, then they'll want to meet the author. And so I take the author round four or five editors, and at that point if everybody's interested, then there'll be an auction. The auction is done from my desk – not with a gavel, it's all just a load of emails and phone calls, trying to get the best deal. I'm always very clear that the author reserves the right not to take the highest offer because quite often they'll meet an editor and they'll get each other. I try and get the best possible deal but with the editor that the author has chosen rather than just letting them go for the money. But some people have said, 'All I want is money, I don't care where I end up as long as it's published.' A lot of times people who really love writing, who really feel that they are writers, might have to work full-time and they might have kids and they are just crying for the time to write. That's what a good deal can buy people, a bit more time to write.

So yeah, then the deal is done and there's much celebrating, and there definitely is a big lunch and lots of drink and lots of cheer. Almost the best moment I have is when I phone a writer and tell them they're going to be published for the first ever time. It is incredibly exciting. In fact I did it this morning, and she was crying and just couldn't believe it. It's brilliant, it is really brilliant. It's only ever going to be downhill from there. It's really, really thrilling and it's kind of heartbreaking how much it means to people. Because writers are all different but they are all incredibly passionate and incredibly emotional.

DAVID: What do all writers have in common?

JO: They all have a mixture of two things that they have to have, almost equally. One is great self-belief, the self-belief that keeps you going when you're on your seventh draft and it's still not there. But also they all have to have great self-doubt because if you don't have self-doubt you're not a creative person. Creative people have to have self-doubt, that's part of their make-up.

DAVID: Why do they have to have self-doubt?

JO: Because I think if you're certain about things, there's a certain flatness to your worldview. You have to be questioning things all the time to work out what you want to say. Even if you're writing a really merry picture book for five year olds, you have to have that.

DAVID: Very often when people find out what I do, they will give me a children's book that they self-published and you can really tell why it wasn't published. It has all the ingredients but it's nothing.

JO: It's linear and it doesn't develop and it doesn't have a shape. Yeah, totally.

DAVID: Unlike *The Tiger Who Came To Tea*...

JO: It's a brilliant book. She's a survivor of Nazi Germany. There is a certain fear around it. It's not a kitten that came to tea.

DAVID: I said to you earlier that my accountant said many of her writer clients were needy compared to her other clients and you said there was some truth in that.

JO: I don't like the word 'needy' because it's so unkind. But it's a pretty lonely process writing and you do need reassurance. You do need to be told that it's worth sitting there at your lonely kitchen table. I've got writers who get up at five in the morning and write for two hours before they go into work, and they're absolutely on their knees in the evening. They need to know that what they're doing is worth doing. Why did you want to write?

DAVID: I just started doing it. I was always writing things. I couldn't stop.

JO: I think that's another thing that all writers have, is a need to do it. They just have to. They can't not do it.

DAVID: It's not a need to make money or be noticed.

JO: No. And when it is, it doesn't work.

DAVID: Describe some characteristics of writers.

JO: There is a certain type who are quite entitled, who feel that they've done the work and now they deserve huge success. And that isn't necessarily how it works. There's chemistry and zeitgeist and timing and luck, and all sorts of things that go into a publication. Some things don't hit and some things do, and that's a hard thing to learn. Some authors think they deserve success but most don't. Most think every piece of good news is a lucky break, but that may be because I'm pretty careful to represent those people. You hear some awful stories about very arrogant and entitled writers. I'd say there are quite a lot who are very, very sensitive and I'm only learning now how careful I need to be.

DAVID: How sensitive? Feeling deeply hurt? Them or their work?

JO: Both. You can have a really merry boozy fun time at the pub, and the next morning they phone you and say, 'You know when you said such and such, did you mean blah blah blah?' There can be a general teasing mood, but a writer will take something personally and worry over it.

DAVID: What do writers want from you?

JO: They want to know that I'm working really hard for them, they want to know that I'm talking to their editors, publicists, marketing people – more often than I actually am. Each author probably wants to feel that they are my only author, but they also like the idea of being in a bunch of successful other people. That's a bit of a tricky one. On the one hand when you've got successful clients, it does give you more clout. But if I talk to an author and say that I've got a huge long list of things I've got to do, they really don't like it. They want to feel that you've got all the time in the world for them.

DAVID: If I go to the butcher, I'm not annoyed if he's on the phone while wrapping up my meat. But if I call my agent and she says she's busy with another client I get annoyed. What's he got that I haven't?

JO: Because it takes it out of people personally so much to write, I feel like it has to be a very personal relationship. It's really hard to separate things out and just go, 'Well, I'm only dealing with your work.'

DAVID: What makes writers angry with you? What makes writers happy with you?

JO: They're happy when I do them a good deal, that's for sure. I think some of them are really pleased if I'm really careful with them and say, 'Don't send out that piece of work until I've done a lot more on it.' They're cross at the time but afterwards they often thank me.

DAVID: The highs of a writer are being accepted by you, and publication. What are other positive things about being your client?

JO: I think it's really hard when you bust a gut and you can sense when there's not a buzz around your book, and people aren't excited and they are excited about something else. It can make people very angry and they can blame me, they can blame their editor, they can blame their publisher, they can blame everything. It's very hard for them to accept that sometimes their book just hasn't hit the spot for whatever reason, and however hard everyone's tried.

DAVID: What is the perfect scenario for a writer's first few books?

JO: Well, the dream is that the first book gets shortlisted for an award, or wins one, the second book follows on and is as interesting if maybe not quite as good, but the third book is better than the first book, and on we go. Some people just storm it and go into the bestseller list and stay there.

DAVID: Is it hard to maintain a career as an author?

JO: Yes it is.

DAVID: Is it harder than ever?

JO: Yes.

DAVID: What creates a buzz? What is a buzz?

JO: It's much more apparent now with social media. About six months before publication, proofs of the book are sent out to so-called opinion makers, so Caitlin Moran or India Knight or Charlie Brooker – people who have a big following on Twitter – will probably be getting, say, thirty books a week. It will also be sent out to book bloggers and other authors. If just a few people say, 'This book is really seriously good,' it makes a difference.

DAVID: Even if people don't actually buy the book, they just Tweet about it.

JO: Exactly. The buzz is a very tangible and yet intangible phenomenon, but I can tell when a book's going to sink without trace just because nobody's picking it up. It's been sent out to all these opinion formers and nobody's been particularly interested.

DAVID: What are your favourite things about your job?

JO: I really, really love doing deals. That is one of the reasons it took me so long to become an agent, because business was a bit of a dirty word in my arty-farty family. I really like doing business, I really like getting someone a better deal than I thought I could. I love being the first reader of something really good. Thinking that nobody has ever read this and knowing that with any luck 50,000 people are going to be shouting about it in a couple of years' time. That's a really exciting feeling. And I love working closely with authors and making them better.

DAVID: You're very hands on. When you see a book in a shop, do you feel that you effectively wrote some of it?

JO: No, but it's very collaborative, I do feel very involved. Some people say, 'It's finished, here it is,' and I might make the odd suggestion, but most authors I work quite closely with. If they say the book is perfect and they're right, that's fine, but if they're not right then I can't sell it. It's a bloody competitive world.

DAVID: The process of getting a book published is complex; there's a lot of people involved all the way down the line.

JO: There's one thing that people say, which is to put a book into the hands of a customer in Waterstones, it needs to have been sold six times. Because you, the author, have sold it to me, the agent, I have sold it to the editor, the editor has sold it to her sales and marketing team, the sales and marketing team have sold it to the book buyers for the chains, the book buyers have sold it on to the individual booksellers and the individual shops, and the book sellers sell it to the customer.

DAVID: Some people are against the idea of agents. They don't see why you should give a percentage of your income to someone who may not sell your work, or who may be greedy or even dishonest…

JO: The idea of a greedy agent or a sharp agent doesn't make sense because I can only make money when my authors make money. I don't earn anything if they don't earn anything. So the idea that an agent is taking your money… There are statistics about self-published authors versus agented authors and you do make more with an agent because they know the tricks of the trade.

DAVID: What five things would you tell an aspiring author?

JO: I'd tell them to write every day. To read more than they write. Don't give up and wait until you find the right person. When your book is as good as it possibly can be, and you're as proud of it as you possibly can be, then don't imagine that the first five people you send it to are necessarily going to read it. You as an author are looking for an agent who's going to have that complete direct response to you. There are hundreds of agents and there may only be one who completely just understands what you're trying to do. If your work is good enough then it shouldn't be a personal thing, it's just about finding that match. A lot of people take that rejection very, very hard when they've done something they're really proud of and the agents aren't getting it, and it may just be that the chemistry isn't right.

DAVID: The idea of giving up is an interesting one because writers can't give up.

JO: You can't give up but you can improve. And you will improve, the more you do it. You'll say, 'Oh, I remember when I got stuck on my last book. How did I fix it last time?'

DAVID: Nobody gets worse by writing.

JO: No, I don't think they do. I think they get better and better.

And on that hopeful note, we finished our Japanese food and went our separate ways, me feeling encouraged and even optimistic. In a harsh commercial world where people put butter on novels and feed them to deer, it's good to know that agents – maligned as they can be – are actually part of the process of making what you write better.

CHAPTER SEVEN

DENNIS KELLY
– 'I Mean This'

How do we spend the middle of our writer's day? Panicking about work? Ploughing on? Posting images of young cats on the internet? For me, the middle of the day, the sluggish afternoon, is normally the time I start to feel a bit slow. I might have a break now, or make some phone calls. I might well be on a train, which is a great place to work. Useful writing tip – everywhere is your office and the worse it is the better. I often write on Southeastern Trains, whose awful rolling stock offers one massive benefit for writers in that it makes no concessions for people who might want to enjoy their journey. No Wi-Fi, no plug sockets, no buffet, and from time to time the odd beguiling stop in the middle of nowhere. Southeastern Trains ensure that you have nothing to distract you from the great task of writing. I put on a pair of headphones – I don't often play music through them, I just use them as earplugs – cram my laptop onto whatever tiny surface I can find, and start writing. You block out the world and you can work.

When I'm not doing that, I'm just sitting back in my seat and letting the feelings flow over me. As a writer, the main feeling that flows over me is generally envy. Envy of other writers and their presumably glittering careers. And if there's one writer whose work is deserving of my envy, it's Dennis

Kelly. His career is extraordinary. He began as a playwright, earning acclaim and fans wherever his work was staged. He went into television as co-writer with Sharon Horgan of one of the few grown-up sitcoms ever made, *Pulling*, and he went into the West End as co-writer with Tim Minchin of the enormous hit, *Matilda: The Musical*. But it is for the Channel 4 series *Utopia* – chilling, funny, bleak and enormously entertaining – that I envy him the most.

Dennis Kelly is an extraordinary writer and I spoke to him on the phone about his writing life. It was, quite frankly, one of the most overwhelming phone conversations I've ever had. Kelly is a passionate man and one reluctant to moderate either his feelings or his language. In a good mood he's effusive, emotional and articulate. I dread to think what he's like in a bad mood: the same, probably.

DAVID: First of all, I wanted to say that I don't know how a human being could write *Utopia*. I think it's amazing.

DENNIS: I was lucky to do it. It's all about who you're working with, really. You've worked with loads of great people, haven't you? I think you've always got to try and work with people who are just a bit better than you and then you've got a chance of doing something good.

DAVID: When do you wake up as a rule?

DENNIS: I have a difficult thing because I am really a morning writer, but the problem is that I'm a night owl. So I'm like a morning person trapped in the body of a late person. I never really sleep before two or three o'clock in the morning and I don't normally get up until about nine, nine thirty or something. So I have this conflict. I write in the evenings as well but I generally think I write a bit better in the morning. I'm less distracted in the morning, I think.

DAVID: Jon Ronson told me that when he was forced to work in the afternoon he found that it wasn't actually that bad. But a lot of people believe that mornings are better for writers.

DENNIS: Yeah, I used to only write in the morning and now I think I've discovered that writing later on isn't too bad. If you write in the morning and you do actually write instead of sitting around scratching your arse or Googling cats or whatever, then you feel better and you're happier. It's as much about being a decent human being. And if you don't get any work done, if you've spent all day farting around, it kind of nags at you and you become a bit grumpy. So I think writing in the morning is good for that reason. But I know people that only write at night and can't write at all during the day. That seems like a strange life. I should be that person, that's who I should be. I'm crap after a certain time. But I can sort of write up until nine or ten o'clock if I need to.

DAVID: It's interesting what you say about the need to write. A lot of people think it's about creative expression but it's actually like the need to go to the toilet. In the sense that it's a compulsion and you feel bad if you don't do it.

DENNIS: Yeah, you get blocked up. It's funny because when people are starting out the question you get asked loads – do you write every day? – you get asked that all the time and it's sort of… Once it becomes your job, you are writing every day because what else would you be doing? You forget how much you wrote back at the beginning, and the time you gave to it was quite an important thing.

At the beginning I would challenge myself. If I found myself on the sofa watching a sitcom that I hated I would be saying, do you want to be a writer or not? Why are you watching something stupid when you're not writing? And actually it was a really good challenge to myself.

When I started out I wrote this play and then I didn't write anything for about two or three years because I was too scared. Then I was with this girl who was a writer and she sort of blew my mind because she would say, 'I'm a writer' even though neither one of us was at the time. I didn't know you could do that, I didn't know you could walk around saying 'I'm a writer' without a written certificate. I thought that was probably illegal. But she surprised me by writing and I realized that the thing I wasn't doing was writing. I was wafting around saying I was a writer or pretending I was a writer but really there's a clue in the title in the job description. If you're not writing then you can't be a writer really. And you have to write and you have to get beyond the thing of how much should I write and stuff like that. You should just do it really.

And I always think there's no such thing as bad writing, the only bad writing is writing that you don't do. Because even the shit stuff you learn from.

DAVID: When you get up in the morning, what do you look forward to?

DENNIS: You mean as a writer or as a human being?

DAVID: Both, they're kind of tied up. But mostly as a writer.

DENNIS: I have inveigled food into my writing process, so a big part of my writing day is lunch, is going out. Near where I live there's quite a nice place where you can get a decent sandwich and a nice coffee and they do stupid good cakes. You know like everywhere has got a trendy coffee shop these days? I discovered years ago that I like writing outside, I like writing in amongst people. My theory on this is that it's just the right amount of being anonymous and also of being seen. You're anonymous because no one gives a shit about you, no one gives a shit about what you're doing – no one in this country gives a shit about anyone else anyway. But also you can't sit there scratching your arse which you can do in a room on your own. I can just stare at a wall. When I was writing *Utopia*, they gave me a little office in Kudos, and it was the perfect office because it was small but had a door and a very big glass window next to it. So the door meant I could shut everyone out and the glass meant I could be seen, there was something that would make me write. I'm easily distracted. If a fly farts in the garden I wanna know about it.

DAVID: This is fascinating because one of the things I'm obsessed with is this nonsense about writers' rules, the desk with the feather in a jar plucked from a phoenix and Ernest Hemingway's old Biro.

DENNIS: I remember when we did *Matilda* I went round to Roald Dahl's house and they showed me to his shed. And the most interesting thing about Roald Dahl's shed is that it's a shed. The lines are all drawn, he's got a beautiful garden, his walk to the shed was absolutely beautiful, you've got these lovely trees, this little avenue and he gets in there and it's a dirty old fucking shed. He used to sit there smoking in this hobbledy old chair and a sleeping blanket he'd tuck himself into when it was winter. There was nothing mystical about it at all, it just was a fucking shed. And from what I understand he used to go and do a set amount of hours and that was it. So he'd sit in his shed, force himself to write and then he was free for the day.

I write a lot by hand, especially if I'm writing for theatre, and I made sure that I used shitty Biros because I didn't want to use a quill. I didn't want to get into that thing that I've got to have my special paper and my special pen. The more you demystify it, the better it is in a way.

DAVID: I've written articles on my phone.

DENNIS: The article's in your brain, isn't it? What I say to young writers at the start is that everything is writing. I think what we're doing right now is writing. The bit where you put the ink on the paper is the tip of the iceberg. I like thinking like that because it frees me up when I'm writing. I don't have to be communing with the gods. What you're doing as a writer is looking at life and figuring some stuff out. If you're writing a comedy you're thinking, 'That's funny, it's funny the way we interact here'.

DAVID: A lot of British comedy writers are all about the line. What I liked about your stuff with Sharon Horgan is that it's about relationships, it's not just setting up for clever wordplay or something.

DENNIS: It's funny, I saw Sharon the other day and we were talking about this. Whenever we got – on the rare occasions – when we got nominated for awards, it was almost impossible to show a clip because it wasn't these funny one-liners. We had a few one-liners, we did a bit of that, but generally it was about the situation. If you look at things like *Steptoe & Son*, those kind of sitcoms, although they have great one-liners, it's totally about the situation, it's totally about what those characters are doing to each other and what that situation is on that day. I think sitcoms have become a bit more 'sketchy' in a way.

DAVID: You work in public, which is very unusual, and also answers my next question about whether or not you play music or watch videos when you work. You can't really do that, you can't get up and have a game of ping pong in a cafe.

DENNIS: No, but the cafe is only one part of it. I'll work in the mornings there, but for some reason lunch has become a thing for me. It's almost like I'm offering myself chocolate if I write. And the animal part of me has learnt, now, not to write unless there's chocolate at the end of it.

Sometimes my office is clean and sometimes it's a total tip. I probably work a bit better when it's clean but I don't have a need for things to be mystical, I don't feel I need to set an atmosphere. At the same time, I don't knock that because I know other people do and some very good writers need to be in a certain space. For me I worked quite hard at not needing those things early on.

DAVID: Do you play music?

DENNIS: No. I'm so easily distracted by music, that's gotta be out.

DAVID: They say it's good for creating an atmosphere.

DENNIS: I can see that though. And I know people who read a lot when they write. I'm the opposite, I tend not to read when I write and because I'm writing all the time now I've kind of stopped reading, which is very bad.

DAVID: Do you find you get really influenced by someone else's voice?

DENNIS: I think that's right. I can find myself getting too close to someone else's voice. I think some of that is not bad. We're all stealing all the time, aren't we? I'm looking at something and I think, that's really good, and I think I'd like to explore that… I think that's valid because what we're doing by writing things is trying to talk about what it's like to be a human being. That's all of us are ever writing about, what this fucking thing is like, what this strange thing is like. When you see someone expressing that quite well, it's natural for you to want to carry on that conversation.

DAVID: It's interesting what you say about us all writing about the human condition because some of what you've done – adaptations of children's stories and horrible dystopias – might arguably be very little to do with humanity.

DENNIS: I would disagree though. Maybe it has little to do with humanity in the sense of being a humane person, but it's a lot to do with being a human being. I think any objective look at our species has to conclude that violence is a massive part of it. Something that frustrates me enormously is the Disneyfication of stories, the idea that things have to go well. I see very little evidence that good triumphs. I think there is massive good in us as people, I think we're an incredible species, we do the most amazing things for each other but we also do the most abominable brutal disgusting things to each other. We do things that you could never put on screen. The stuff on the news or in the average newspaper, you would never see a fraction of that on screen. With *Utopia* we got a bit of stick for doing a school shooting even though you didn't see any violence in that school shooting. But I think since that there've been something like 200 similar shootings in America.

I would always hope that I try not to revel in the bad stuff. I just think how can we talk about ourselves if we don't talk about it?

DAVID: *Matilda* is rather the flipside of *Utopia* in that it's a little bit more surreal, more comic-like.

DENNIS: Yeah it is. It's a bit more cartoon. I wrote the book of the musical. I was a bit cynical about musicals before but now I feel musicals can be amazing. I think often they're not because a lot of producers get a book writer in at the end to glue the songs together. What the RSC did was different, they got the book writer in at the beginning. I think that's the right way to do it. The only way I can describe it is that *Matilda* is drawn in crayon, but that doesn't mean it has to be a bad picture. You can use bright colours and you can talk about exactly the same things.

That's the thing about Dahl. He does actually talk about what it's like to be a person. What he doesn't do is pretend that he's a decent person. He doesn't walk around pretending he's some good guy that can hand out life lessons, which is what we often do as authors… You often get asked, 'What do you want to teach people with your writing?' I don't want to teach anyone anything. I'm not a moral person. I think I'm vaguely moral, but I'm still a twat and I've got no desire to teach.

DAVID: What methods do you use to generate ideas?

DENNIS: I don't know. It's a variety of things. I recently stopped doing things that people came to me with because I was a bit scared that I'd lose my idea generating muscle… The hard thing is not having ideas. First off it's seeing them through and then it's being able to understand whether what you've written is any good or not.

DAVID: Have you ever written something that you thought was good but wasn't? Or vice versa?

DENNIS: Oh definitely, yeah. I try not to think that anything's good. Even things that I've done well, I try not to think of them as good and I try not to think of things I haven't done well as bad. I sort of think that that sort of stuff is none of my fucking business. My business is to write it and to write it as well as I can. This notion of it being good or bad is something that's a bit dangerous for writers.

But there's another thing about whether things are working or not. You have to be honest with yourself about whether what you want to say is coming across. Because that's the thing that you'll lie to yourself about. Or whether what you want to say is as interesting as you think it is. It might be very interesting for you but not for everyone else in the world. It's about recognizing those things.

DAVID: How much do you revise?

DENNIS: I would try to hand in as complete a thing as I can do at that moment but I also recognize that I'm not always capable – in that moment – of making it as complete as it should be. I like to rewrite. I think Hemingway said the first draft of everything is shit. I like that. I like to have permission to write bad things. It relaxes me. I get to a moment where I feel a bit scared and I'll write in another book because I'll pretend to myself that I'm just messing around. I've been doing this for about fifteen years and I still fall for that trick – I end up with a play in about five different books.

DAVID: Are you writing literally your life? Is it your livelihood?

DENNIS: Yeah, it is a lot to me. I mean, it's my livelihood, but it's not just a job. I made a rule when I started out that I'd never write just for the money. Don't get me wrong: I'm very happy when people give me money, but I've never taken a job for the money. I think it's stood me in good stead thinking like that. It's definitely more than just a job for me. I had a big drink problem and getting sober and work are sort of intertwined for me. They're very close those things and my writing career really dates from when I started getting sober.

I'm quite against most writing courses even though I've never been on one. I don't know why, I've got a slight pathological hatred of them. It's a terrible thing because I know lots of people who teach them and they're really lovely people. I even speak on them… My worry is that they'll twat around and tell you stuff about character and structure and blah blah blah and who gives a shit about any of that? You figure that out. What's difficult is what you're talking about, which is what does it feel like writing? How do you deal with your ego? How do you deal with your fear? How do you deal with the strange swarms of emotions that roll through your stupid writer's brain? And how do you get past that so you can write something that's honest?

DAVID: Yes, I've just persuaded 500 people to crowd-fund a novel and I keep thinking, what if it's shit?

DENNIS: Your only defence against stuff like that is your honesty. It's your only defence against all of it. That is scary, putting it up for lots of people you don't know to say shit things about you – not just things you've written, shit things about *you*. They can get personal and your only defence is to be honest. Our tendency is to hide and to be clever. To hide in being clever. I personally have got a bit of a hatred of irony. This idea of being postmodern ironic fucks me off because it's a way of saying something and at the same time saying, 'I don't mean that'. It's so cowardly. What we need to say is, 'I mean this. Call me a prick if you want, but I believe in this.'

DAVID: Does a piece of work ever really end?

DENNIS: It's weird isn't it? When we did *Matilda*, Tim and I were really nervous and the director Matthew Warchus said, 'What you've got to remember is that press night is a record of where we've got to at this moment'. And he was right because we carried on working on it after then and after we opened in New York. There's nothing that I look at and think 'that is a perfect thing'. But also I'm never tempted to go back. I think it's probably true that things aren't ever quite finished, but at the same time you have to walk away from them and let them be what they wanna be.

DAVID: I hate 'director's cuts'. For me, the thing that actually comes out on sale is the only version, not someone's remix or re-edit.

DENNIS: It's funny isn't it? People want to do different versions. I'm never intrigued watching alternative endings or DVD exclusives, I just want to watch the thing.

DAVID: What makes you doubt what you do and what makes you think you might be good?

DENNIS: Over the years I've trained myself to not get involved in thinking about something being a success. *Matilda* was in the West End for about a year before I'd even use that word with it. It's not a weird false modesty thing. If you allow yourself to drift off into dreams of your greatness, if you let it get away with you, you just crash afterwards and you stop writing. The same is true of the other thing, of thinking too negatively about yourself. If you allow yourself to think too negatively about yourself, it stops you writing.

I do have doubts, Like most writers, I'm probably more on the doubts side than the good side. It's hard, isn't it? The doubts are generally wildly irrational and so when they come along, they are things like, 'Everyone hates you and you're never going to write a decent word again.' I don't know if I am good, but I think what I've always had is that right from the beginning I thought, 'I might not be good enough to write this but I'm gonna fucking have a go.' I find people are quite scared about writing things. I might not be the greatest writer in the world but I will throw myself at it. I'm quite happy to risk failure, I'm quite happy to risk looking like a real dick. That does mean that I'll do a musical, for example, which as someone who was supposed to be a serious playwright…

DAVID: So many great writers actually do a lot of wide-ranging stuff.

DENNIS: It's an odd thing that we compartmentalize the thing, we say, 'You're a comedy writer, therefore you must write comedy,' or 'you write children's novels therefore you must only write children's novels.' As people who watch things we have a really broad range of tastes. I've very rarely met people who've said, 'I'm only interested in Italian neo-realism film,' and if you do meet those people you stay away from them really. We've all got eclectic tastes.

DAVID: It's like if you went to J.K. Rowling's house and found that she only read novels for twelve year olds, and was only now getting into detective novels.

DENNIS: But weirdly we do have that view with making stuff. There are people who say you only really make one good piece of work, and you continue to make it. And you look at Chekhov and I suppose that's true. But there's different ways of doing things.

DAVID: It's an old argument – one that for me relates to being a hack versus being a true creative. Do you stick to the same idea, honing it and honing it, in the same voice for the entirety of your writing career? Or can you flit from genre to genre, from style to style, and still retain whatever it is that makes your work different from everyone else's?

DENNIS: I remember when I started out people kept talking about voice. I'm really glad that I never really believed in that. It's probably right that people have a particular voice but when you go out on a search to find your voice, that's weird. You come back and go, 'This is my voice' – well, it clearly isn't because you had to go out and search for it. Surely your voice is what you naturally say? Again it's that honesty thing.

And hopefully that would come out if you were doing a drama on TV but also that would come out if you were doing a small film about people living on the Mongolian Steppe, and if you were doing a song that might come out. Because you're you.

DAVID: When you start writing, is it always true that your voice emerges?

DENNIS: The thing is that it needs to be your voice. It's who you are and if it's not, it's gonna be fake. You do run the risk of people not being interested in who you are. But fuck it, it's you at least…

DAVID: And finally, why write? Why bother?

DENNIS: There's lots of other things you can do, we don't have to be writers… I used to think to myself when I was starting out that I wouldn't let writing misbehave. If it wasn't gonna work out, I wasn't going to stay at it for twenty years and be in a world of hell. Writing can be excruciating, it can be a very painful thing, and it can be very difficult.

DAVID: It's very tiring.

DENNIS: Yeah. It is.

CHAPTER EIGHT

MARTYN WAITES AND MARK BILLINGHAM
– 'Darkness Seems To Suit What We're Writing'

G enre fiction is both derided and devoured in equal proportions. People who can't write like sneering at it and people who appreciate good writing like reading it. Genre fiction encompasses a billion varieties, from romance to science fiction, and in those categories, as in every other branch of fiction, there are geniuses and there are idiots.

Which brings me to my next pair of interviewees. They're geniuses, obviously, in the incredibly competitive, varied and exciting world of crime fiction. Mark Billingham is the creator of the Tom Thorne novels and possibly my favourite living crime writer. His work makes you share Thorne's every hangover and crime scene fag. He's also extremely funny, as befits a former stand-up (and he was Gary in *Maid Marian and Her Merry Men*). Martyn Waites is equally entertaining in company as well as being a great writer. In fact, he's two great writers, working under his own name and as Tania Carver (and, like Mark, he's done some acting, appearing amongst other things in *The New Adventures of Robin Hood*). Together with Stav Sherez, another top-notch crime writer who was supposed to be in this interview but sadly couldn't make it (and so far as I can tell has never done any Sherwood Forest-related acting), Mark, Martyn and I wrote a book called *Great Lost Albums*, which is one of the most hilarious comedy and rock books ever written. It really is.

I met Mark and Martyn in the dining area of a West End club and we got straight into it.

DAVID: OK, it's a day in the life. What time do you wake up and start thinking about the day?

MARTYN: I like being a late riser but I'm an early waker. I can usually wake up at seven or something like that and read for a bit. Reading for a bit gets me in the mood to write.

MARK: You read in the morning? I'm a reasonably early waker. I like to lie in as long as humanly possible. It tends not to happen with dogs and kids and all that kind of stuff. It always has a knock-on effect for me because I work late, I'm a late writer.

DAVID: So what do you do? You get up, you've got families of varying degrees. How do you start your day?

MARK: It's always admin. Emails that have come in overnight, emails that can be work-related or nutter-related. 'Why isn't there a cat in the TV adaptation of this book? There was a cat in the book and there's no cat on the TV version and I'm disgusted and let down.' You're dealing with the stuff that anybody else has to deal with. Cats and accounts and whatever else it might be, and in a way it sets you up for the day. You look at all the websites you visit that are vaguely connected, all the crime fiction type stuff. And Twitter obviously, you have your little morning fix of Twitter, which is how you find out if somebody's died and it's often where you get your news from.

MARTYN: One of the first things I do is check Twitter. But then you've got feeds set up… like news feeds and the Bookseller feeds which are set up on Twitter so if there's any publishing news that you need to know about, like you're suddenly without an editor or a publisher… You always check that and it's very hard not to fall down that rabbit hole and get distracted by that to the extent that you don't do anything else. But I also try to, as Mark says, take care of the admin. I'm shit at answering emails, I'm shit at dealing with anything like that.

MARK: I'm very diligent about answering every email, every Tweet. Because it's easy to do. I'm sure in the days when writers had quills and parchment it was harder but now it's so easy.

DAVID: If you'd been writers at your sort of level of success in the 1970s, what do you think your morning would have been like?

MARK: Newspapers, empty bottles of port and that kind of thing. Crime writers back in those days had a reputation for being sort of lashed. I think with Alistair MacLean there were prostitutes he needed to send home in the morning.

MARTYN: Eric Ambler. You can say that 'cos they're dead.

MARK: Looking at and writing for blogs, that's kind of at a tangent from actually writing the book stuff. You've got to write an article for WH Smith, or some bookseller somewhere says, 'Can you contribute to that blog?' or whatever it might be. Those kinds of things where you're sort of getting the writing muscles working without actually being that creative.

DAVID: I have a hierarchy. So if I'm going to write a film script, I'll do some record reviews first. It's like a warm up.

MARK: Just getting used to typing…

MARTYN: You do an article like My Top Ten Crime Novels.

MARK: Yes, Top Ten Favourite Books, The Books By My Bedside, all those things that you get asked to do all the time. Which often you can just cut and paste from something you wrote ten years before. My ten favourite books probably haven't changed that much in the past ten years…

MARTYN: But also I often feel that I can't start writing until I've got all that out of the way. That's like the niggle in the background, that's like the thing that will stop you concentrating and stop you fully committing to work.

DAVID: It's like needing the loo isn't it?

MARTYN: Yeah. I can't remember which writer it was who said, 'How do you start a novel? The first thing I do is to defrost the freezer.' I find that the whole day is like that. I have to play games on the computer. I have to check the Newcastle United website. This becomes the kind of ritual that you do. And then you've got to deal with all the correspondence and stuff and the accountant stuff and the agent stuff and anybody else like that. If I start writing straight away and I do maybe 1000 words in the morning, I always think, 'It's rubbish'. Even if it's not, I always think it will be because I distrust the fact that I've started straight away. And I'll try and pull that apart.

MARK: That thing of thinking that what you're writing is rubbish is hugely important. If I am going to go, 'Right, now time for the book' and I open up the document, the current work in progress, the first thing I do is read rather than write, so I go back over what I wrote the day before. And that's when you go, 'It's unpublishable rubbish' and you hit the delete button a lot. And that used to really worry me until I spoke to other writers who went, 'No, we always think it's rubbish.' Any time you talk to a writer and you go, 'How's the new book going?' and they say 'Great,' you think, 'That's a really bad sign, that's probably going to be a dog of a book.'

DAVID: So every time you open the file you think, 'I have to rewrite this'?

MARTYN: Yeah, I always look at the day before's stuff. Because I know what I was thinking when I wrote it and I know what I was trying to get across and I know that the goals that I had them might not have been the goals that it actually needed. Like maybe I've got to get my word count up because that's what I've got to do today, so I can allow myself to relax a bit.

MARK: It's also where something like Twitter actually can be quite useful for once. It's great for bits of gossip and scandal and jokes and all that kind of stuff. But when you tweet something like, 'I'm halfway through this book and it's kicking my arse,' you'll get fifty tweets back from other writers going, 'Yeah, me too.' There is a kind of strange support system at work. We love to see another writer going, 'This is terrible.'

DAVID: You can't imagine Raymond Chandler writing to Dashiell Hammett…

MARK: And then a week later he gets a telegram from Hammett. And a picture of a cat.

MARTYN: Laugh out loud.

MARK: You're a very disciplined writer, Martyn. You put autoreply on your emails saying, 'I'm on radio silence.' I will just write for ten minutes until an email pings and I'll go 'Oh email!' I'm very easily distracted.

MARTYN: But I always have to put my Freedom For Mac on when I'm sitting at my desk. It's a computer programme that ensures you don't get any emails and you can't go online. But then if I'm really desperate for distraction I'll get the laptop out or the iPad. It's almost like you should find somebody to hide the computer for you so that you're not distracted too much.

DAVID: Why doesn't anybody just get a laptop without the internet on it?

MARTYN: A writing laptop? It would be the best thing to do.

MARK: That is what all these programmes are replicating.

MARTYN: A dark room with a bag over your head…

DAVID: My dad would say, 'I've got a machine that does that already…it's called a typewriter'.

MARTYN: Absolutely right.

MARK: But the big myth about writing is that it only happens when you're in front of a screen or you've got a piece of paper in front of you. Writing happens when you're pushing the trolley round the supermarket or driving the kids to school or walking the dogs. That's when the book you're working on is in your head all the time.

MARTYN: You know the old variety acts, the plate spinners? They'd start off with one plate spinning on a stick, then another one, then another one, they'd have about thirty or forty plates spinning and keep having to check which one was spinning and which one was about to fall off. That's pretty much what it's like to write a novel. Those plates, those thirty or forty plates, are still spinning in your head the whole time and you've got to make sure that not one of those plates swivels and falls off.

DAVID: Are you able to freeze frame? You're writing and you stop then you come back to the place where you left off writing.

MARK: Sometimes you actually have to stop and walk away, because in crime fiction there's a lot of problem solving involved in complex plots and you get to a point where you've written yourself into a corner and you can't just write through that, you go, 'I have to solve this problem that I've made.' And you may solve that in the shower, you go, 'Oh God, I know exactly how he's going to get out of that.' And sometimes your family have been talking to you for ten minutes, and you've not been listening because you're trying to figure out how to get yourself over that wall and suddenly the answer appears. And it's also about trying to hold the structure of something that's 120,000 words long in your head. Because if you're too close, it's all about not being able to see the wood for the trees. And even when you write 'The End' you've got to hand it over to somebody else who goes, 'There's ten chapters in the middle that go nowhere,' because you're just way too close to it to be able to figure it out.

DAVID: How can you not notice that?

MARK: Well, I think that you do, really. When you look at it again, you feel that there's something that's not right. It's that tiny little voice of doubt in your head that goes, 'Does that character really work?' You hand it over and your editor says, 'I'm not sure that character works,' and straight away you go, 'Yes I knew that.' Most of the time that little voice in your head is right.

DAVID: Let's talk about criticism. Do you welcome it or do you dismiss it out of hand?

MARK: I think there are some writers who do that, but I absolutely don't. This goes back to my days as a stand-up. If I'm onstage at the Comedy Store and 599 people are wetting themselves, all I'm thinking about is the bald guy at the front who's just staring at me.

DAVID: Why?

MARK: I don't know why. That's all you care about. 'I've got to make you laugh.' So you get ten reviews for your book and if nine of them are glowing and one's a slagging, it's the slagging you remember and the slagging that makes you go, 'Yeah you're right.'

MARTYN: It's a cliché that the only reviews you remember are the bad ones, but they are.

DAVID: You're saying that the only reviews you agree with are the bad ones?

MARTYN: I think that says a lot about how writers often see themselves.

MARK: I think that's changed in recent years because the majority of reviews are written by amateur reviewers. The majority of reviews are on Amazon and looking at

Amazon reviews is just a sure way to drive yourself insane. It's bonkers. 'I had this book delivered and when I opened it the jacket was torn' – one star. 'I borrowed this book from the library and I had to take it back before I finished it' – one star. There's a lot of them written by conspiracy theorists.

DAVID: So you tend to agree with people who critique your work, all the way down the line from your partner to your editor?

MARK: Every reader's opinion counts, whether they're a professional critic or somebody that's read the book and wants to send you an email. Because a book is just a thing, a yellowing manuscript or a file on your computer, until somebody reads it. And anything anybody says when they read it, whatever axe they've got to grind, whether they like it or they hate it, counts for something. You can choose to ignore it or you can let it keep you awake at night, but it has to count for something.

DAVID: You're saying your book's a functional thing, like a motorbike or a bicycle.

MARK: Absolutely, you're right. You can be sitting reading it on the tube or the bus and perhaps somebody that you're sitting next to filters into the description of the character that you're reading, so that becomes a reader's individual experience of reading that. You write a comedy sketch and you look at it on paper or on the screen and go, 'I'm very pleased with that,' but the proof of the pudding is when that sketch is transmitted and somebody laughs or doesn't laugh. It doesn't count until that happens. I think that's true of any piece of art.

I really distrust writers who say, 'I write for myself.' We are both commercial writers, we write because we are paid to write, that's our job and therefore I'm trying to do a performance to a reader, I'm trying to entertain. And 'entertain' meaning a lot of different things – laugh, cry, gasp – whatever it might be, all that stuff.

MARTYN: I don't want to let the reader down. I don't want to disappoint the reader, I don't want somebody to have paid for this and not like it. You get emails, you see people look forward to the books coming out, and the book is often something that they'll buy ahead of time.

MARK: They read it overnight, they read it in twelve hours and get straight back to you the next day. Somebody has taken the time in their life to get excited about something that we've built and so you have a responsibility and an obligation not to disappoint them.

DAVID: Some writers say they write because they've got something to say. Surely it's about telling the best story that you can tell?

MARK: But you can still say what you want within that. One of the things I love about the crime novel is that you've got your beginning, middle and end, it's not too rigid a structure but it has to be a recognisable followable structure that your reader will trust that you'll deliver.

DAVID: A structure that everybody's used from the snootiest writers to the worst writers – it seems that everyone's done a crime story.

MARK: You do feel – not that you're standing on the shoulders of giants or something – but that you are part of a tradition. We're members of the Detection Club, a club that was founded by Agatha Christie and Dorothy L. Sayers, and we're writing in the same tradition of these amazing writers. People like crime fiction and there are certain boxes you have to tick and we can do what we can to try and move that forward and maybe try different things. But nobody makes you be a crime writer, nobody's put a gun to your head. If you don't like it, don't do it.

My pet hate is people who are clearly writing crime fiction who then go, 'No no no, I'm playing with the tropes, I'm subverting the genre, and I'm transcending the genre'. The genre doesn't need transcending. Why not do something else? It's not compulsory.

MARTYN: How many times do you go along to an event and see a panel of new writers talking and a large amount of them say, 'Oh I didn't realize I was writing a crime novel'?

MARK: I was on a panel this year where three out of four writers went, 'I didn't realize I was writing a crime novel.' And the chair of the panel said, 'Did the dead body not give you a clue?'

DAVID: Can we talk about genre fiction? When you write genre fiction, you allow yourself to be guided by the rules of the genre. You're not going to have a poem halfway through the book, you're not going to have a scene where the corpse speaks or a dragon comes in. What are the pros and cons of this?

MARTYN: Of genre writing? Well, I'm making sticks that – air quotation marks – 'literary writers' will beat other writers with. I think the reason that people don't like genre fiction is because they look down on it as some kind of inferior thing. But you can tell a story, involve the reader in a way that makes them care about characters and what happens to them...

MARK: I heard a radio review recently where they were reviewing *The Girl On the Train*...

MARTYN: ... the latest crime novel to 'transcend the genre'.

MARK: ... Somebody said, 'I thought the characters were a bit weak,' and somebody else went, 'You don't need strong characters in a crime novel.' And strong characters are the most important thing in any novel. Yes, there's got to be a certain box-ticking about plot twists and resolutions and all that kind of stuff, but you've got to have characters readers care about.

DAVID: Kazuo Ishiguro recently said that a lot of people buy his books to make themselves look good. Like carrying the sleeve of a cool album under your arm.

MARK: It's only in this country that that kind of snobbery exists. It certainly doesn't happen elsewhere in Western Europe. You go to France or Scandinavia, they take crime fiction very seriously. You don't just get asked, 'Where do you get your ideas from,' or, 'Why have you got nice embossed jackets?'

MARTYN: I love going to France. You write stuff here and you're ignored, but you write stuff in France and you're considered a serious literary writer.

DAVID: Returning to the increasingly vague theme of this book – what do you do at lunchtime?

MARK: You have a sandwich, you watch the one o'clock news.

MARK: It's a very, very rare thing to not be at home. Which means you spend all day in your dressing gown, which is great in one sense when your kids bring friends home from school and they look at you and go, 'What does your dad do?' You think: what is the point in getting dressed? I'm very comfortably in my pyjama bottoms and my dressing gown, I'm not going out, all I'm doing is writing. By the time it gets to four o'clock I think that's me done for the day, I'm ready for bed.

MARTYN: They're called 'lounging trousers'.

DAVID: Do you think that people who like hanging around in pyjamas all day become writers because people who don't like to get up early seek jobs where you don't have to do that?

MARTYN: A mate of mine say there's a very thin line between being self-employed and unemployed.

MARK: The weird thing is when you get to the middle of the afternoon, it's like the day's got away from you a bit. Because by then you've got kids coming home from school, so suddenly you've got to deal with domestic family stuff. This is why I write late. I don't know if the same is true of Martyn, but I will be much more productive after the kids have gone to bed, the house is dark, and I'm looking out the window and I can't see anything.

DAVID: You are literally the only people I've talked to who are late writers.

MARK: One of the things about writing later on is that darkness seems to suit what we're writing. When you're looking out the window and it's a nice day and there are birds, it's really hard to concentrate on writing something really dark. When I'm staring out the window at nothing...

DAVID: So when do you start hunkering down and properly writing?

MARTYN: I start at about midnight.

MARK: Sometimes I put it off, I'll go to the gym for a couple of hours because I often find that if you do something physical, it frees your mind up so you can think better. At my old house I need to take the dog for a four mile walk and the constant movement would allow me to think more about the book. And now I'll go to the gym and I'll spend an hour on the cycling or the cross trainer. The day might solve a few problems for me and I'll sit down and I'll get a day's work done in two hours.

MARTYN: When I sit down at night I always feel this huge sigh of relief. It's like you take a deep breath and you've held this breath in all day and you can just sit there in the dark on your own and sigh. I used to take the laptop down to the dining room table and stick a bottle of whisky at the end and that was going to be my treat, to have a drink, when I was finished. I'd sit there and I'd think, 'I've got to do 2000 words before I can have a whisky.' And you get there by about two or three in the morning.

MARK: If I start at midnight, I can go, 'Today I've been a good dad and a good husband and I've put the rubbish out and I've paid the gas bill and I've done all the things that normal people need to do. Now I can just work without other things pulling my attention.' I'm quite obsessed with Flann O'Brien. He was a senior Irish civil servant, he was looking after his family and his sister's family. Worked all day and at night came home pissed from the pub and worked. But he did the day job first. The thing you have to remember is that 95% of published writers have other jobs. Working all day as doctors and teachers and bar staff and whatever, they're the ones that get up at five in the morning and write for a couple of hours, or come home after a full day at work and write for a couple of hours, and still manage to publish novels. They're the writers you really need to respect…

DAVID: Before you'd actually written Chapter One on a piece of paper, who were you?

MARTYN: I was an actor so the idea of work routines was alien. I worked for a telemarketing company, I worked in a call centre in between acting jobs and that was where I started writing novels. I'd do a day's work there, I'd get up at half six and go to work, I'd go in early so I could have coffee and sit and read a book for an hour because I was determined not to have the whole day being about that. And then I'd come back – we had young kids at the time – and I would be with them until about half nine, then I'd start work. Then I'd work through until about one, finish at one then I'd be up at half six again. I did that for five years.

DAVID: Very disciplined.

MARTYN: It didn't feel like I was being disciplined at the time… It's part of the advice that they always give you at drama school: don't do the job you love. If you have to do a job between acting, do a job you hate. That's what I did. I was skint a lot of the time but I never gave up. It's not, 'Don't give up your dreams.' It wasn't a fucking dream, it was hard work. My first two books, I got two grand for each one, that was the reality of it. People kept telling me, 'You got a really good deal there.' Honestly, you think so?

DAVID: A lot of people think two grand is a lot of money for a book. It's not.

MARK: The average advance is still less than ten grand. You might have to live on that for a year so that's why writers have other jobs.

MARTYN: And of course you don't get it in one go.

MARK: Whatever your advance is, whether it's ten grand or a million, you get a quarter when you sign the contract, you get a quarter when you deliver the book, a quarter on paperback allocation, a quarter on hardback allocation. That's two years. That's why I'm particularly passionate about why writers need to get paid for things like festival appearances. There are quite a few high profile festivals with funding coming out of their arses, who don't pay, which is disgusting. It's just outrageous. It wouldn't be applied to anyone else you can think of. You're paid for your time and your expertise. Some festival in, let's say, Wales, that's a day or two days of your life. A day and a half at least. And you're there trying to do the best thing you can, the best performance you can give, there are people who have paid good money to see you, and you won't get paid for it? It's outrageous.

MARTYN: But also – I do think this is an interesting point – everywhere has got a literary festival now, everyone can try and entice writers to get there as well. And if you go you have to present information about yourself in a way that is palatable to get people to read the book, in the same way that you do on social media. You're being

Martyn Waites™, you're being that person that you want people to meet, and it's tiring. Somebody said to me, 'You always seem to be cheerful and always smiling,' and I said, 'Yeah, it takes a fuck of a lot of effort to do this.'

MARK: If you're going to these things there's no point going and being miserable, uncooperative or unfriendly. You're just going to piss off all the people who come to see you, who are going to take one look at you and go, 'I'm not reading his books.'

MARTYN: It's true. The audience don't want to know about how long you've been in therapy or if you're on antidepressants.

MARK: In these days when the novel is threatened, the death of the printed book and all that, there's never been such an appetite for meeting writers in the flesh. People do seem to want to see writers, go out and meet them and give feedback and all that kind of stuff. And I love it. I've come to say that – and probably most writers wouldn't say that – but for me the actual writing is the least endurable part of the job. For me, the perk of the job is going to these things and getting to show off. I love it.

DAVID: One thing I found when I went to a crime-writing festival is that the crime writers are very likable.

MARK: To a degree there's a gang mentality. There's a slight feeling that we're sort of on the periphery so we all need to stick together. The cliché is that we get all of our badness out on the page, which is why we're all sort of happy go lucky.

MARTYN: But also I think it's going back to the idea of genre fiction. A friend of mine who published several crime novels was snapped up by a literary publisher, so the first thing they said is, 'You're a literary novelist, you're not a crime writer anymore.' He said, 'So what does that mean?' and they said, 'Well, a book a year, you won't be doing that any more. That's what crime writers do.' And he said, 'But that's how long it takes me,' and they said, 'Yeah, well, you don't tell people that.' He said, 'What am I going to do in the meantime because it takes me a year to write a book, what am I going to do?' and they said, 'I don't know but you can't write another book in that time because we have to make it seem literary.' The inference being if it's literary, it's hard work, whereas if it's crime, you're just dashing something off. He said he went with that because they paid him to. At the same time he started writing thrillers under a pseudonym because he had nothing to do in his spare time.

DAVID: Talking of pseudonyms… Martyn, you write as yourself and as Tania Carver. How do you work as two different people?

MARTYN: I write under the name Tania Carver – I don't dress up – and I write under my own name, and I do think there is a difference in the styles. There's a difference in the accent on characters and action as well in both of them.

DAVID: Do you mentally dress up as Tania Carver?

MARTYN: Yeah. I can tell what goes in a Tania book and what goes in a Martyn book. It becomes kind of instinctive. I started the novel before last thinking, 'This is a Martyn novel, it's not a Tania novel.' So I put it aside and started a Tania one instead.

DAVID: Iain Banks wrote science fiction under the slightly different name of Iain M Banks, but he did so, I believe, because he was asked by his publishers to separate his 'serious' novels from his SF novels.

MARK: Iain quite famously would spend nine months of the year doing nothing. Nine months travelling around, drinking whisky, enjoying himself, having a good time. Then he'd write a book in three months.

DAVID: If somebody was trying to write your books, what would you tell them to do?

MARK: I would tell them to have a strong opening that is almost like the pre-title sequence of a movie, something to engage the reader very quickly. It's that simple: you've got to engage the reader really quickly. Doesn't necessarily need to be crash bang wallop, some huge high-concept thing, it doesn't have to be blood spattered everywhere. It can just be a voice, it can just be something that piques the reader's interest, so that at the end of that first three or four pages they're going, 'What? Who?' Lots of questions. And at the time of writing you find your questions too. I haven't got anything planned out, I don't really know where it's going from there. Some writers will plot absolutely everything out, they will spend ten months writing an outline and two months writing the book.

I write a book every year, that's not writing every day. I haven't written a word now for about three weeks. But I've got it in my head, I kind of know where I'm going. So you work to your own calendar, but in terms of a method it's – I don't know whether any of the other writers have said this – it's like driving through fog at night. I know where I'm going, I know what the destination is, but I can only see as far as the end of my headlights. So I'm going to take an awful lot of wrong turns, a lot of dead ends, but I'll get there in the end, but it's quite an interesting drive.

DAVID: Why do you write? Some people see writers of genre fiction as mercenary hacks.

MARK: This mercenary idea is a really interesting thing. We've all sat on panels where you get asked, 'Why do you write?' And I've sat with people going, 'Because if I didn't I would die, my soul would shrivel,' and I'm sitting next to them, thinking, 'I'm not like that.' I think the question you need to ask every writer is: if the book is written and optioned for a movie and becomes a huge movie franchise for a zillion dollars, are you going to get up tomorrow and carry on writing? And I'm not really sure I would. Somebody said anybody who writes for anything other than money is a fool. All the writers that I respect – Raymond Chandler, Graham Greene – they wrote for money and they treated it so that it had the discipline that went with a job of work. But it wasn't like they wrote because ideas came down like fairy dust and they just had to.

DAVID: Are you quite contemptuous of the fairy dust school?

MARK: Yes, completely. What they do is deliberately try to make writing sound like it's something very special, like it's something mystical the facility for which only lies with a few people. The idea that it's some weird mystical thing and ideas come down like fairy dust and you hear voices and you channel them, is just nonsense.

DAVID: When you're a writer there's always a suspicion among other people that you are just pissing about.

MARK: That's a suspicion that dogs a lot of writers, even domestically. You know this yourself. Your partner comes in and unless they actually see your fingers flying across the keyboard, they wonder what are you actually doing? I think there's something to be said for the app that gives your keyboard the sound of an old fashioned typewriter. At least they can hear the noise of writing going on. It is quite tricky, especially when the book is actually being sorted out in your head most of the time…

DAVID: Would you carry on writing if you didn't have to?

MARTYN: I don't know what I'd do instead though. I'd have to do something.

MARK: Somebody must have said this, but the best quote of all time is when somebody asked Dorothy Parker if she enjoyed writing, she said, 'I enjoy having written.' That is just so true.

DAVID: In *How to Write Everything*, I've got Dan Brown saying it.

MARK: I wouldn't want to read him. But I'm not going to diss anybody who wants to read Dan Brown or EL James, I hate that kind of snobbery.

DAVID: OK, I'm a total snob about literature and I can't tell your books from Dan Brown's or EL James's. In what way are you two not EL James and Dan Brown?

MARK: Unless you are a complete moron or a psychopath, nobody is setting out trying to write a bad book. Nobody. I'm trying to write the best book that I can.

MARTYN: 'If I'd known the *Da Vinci Code* was going to be so successful, I'd have made it better.' He did say that. Bless him, fair play.

MARK: One of the slight cons of being a genre writer is the fan base want the next book to be pretty much the same as the last one. Just a little bit different. Not too different. But at the same time, within those constraints of the genre you're still trying to write the best book you can. You won't always. There comes a point where you say. 'You know what? That's as fast as I can fucking run. That's it, I've done it, and it's never going to get any better.'

And we haven't mentioned the very weird thing that happens, which is that you finish a book and give a big sigh, you go through all your edits and the job's done and you take a few weeks off. You think, 'I'm fine, the next book isn't due until end of next year.' And you sit down to start the next one and it's like you've never written anything before in your life. It's utterly bizarre. You stare at this thing and it's like you've forgotten how to write. Even if you've written fifteen, sixteen, twenty books, it's only after about one hundred pages that you start to go 'Oh yeah, I think I can do this again.' But every writer I know has that feeling of 'Shit, I've been found out, I can't do it again.'

MARTYN: Also, mistrust any writer who says they enjoy writing.

MARK: Don't get me wrong, it's still the best job in the world, but it's still a job at the end of the day. It's not digging a ditch…The writers I really despise are the ones that talk about writing like that. There was an interview with Jeffrey Archer in *Time Out* and he really did say, 'At the end of the day I'm drained,' and I'm thinking, 'He's not digging a ditch.' Digging a ditch is the only job that's like digging a ditch. But the things that go with it in this day and age, I enjoy more. I think for writers from a different generation it would be like putting pins in their eyes to stand up in front of an audience and talk about their work?

I think if you have any degree of a performance background or performance savvy, these kind of things are great. Give me a room with 500 people and twenty minutes and I will persuade them to buy my book.

DAVID: What do you think are the universals for writers? What have you got in common with writers in general?

MARK: When I was twelve I wrote a story in school, 'What I Did In My Holidays,' whatever it was. I just tried to write the funniest story that I could and the teacher said, 'Mark, do you want to come to the front of the class and read your story out?' And the buzz of that… I can still remember how viscerally excited I was. Twenty-nine other kids in the class, reading my story to them. That's why I write, essentially, and that's what I think I have in common with most of the writers I respect.

I'm just trying to tell a story to as many people as possible and to make it as good as I possibly can. I think that, if at some level there isn't part of that in what you do, I really don't know why you're a writer.

MARTYN: I was shit at school writing stories. My teachers always used to say they were terrible.

MARK: You used to sit down at the back of the class and read your story.

And with that, we had a drink and we left.

CHAPTER NINE

ISZI LAWRENCE
– 'Stand-Up Is A Conversation'

Not all writing is designed to be read. A lot of it – acting, stand-up, presenting – is intended to be spoken, frequently by the person who wrote it. Unsurprisingly, this kind of writing brings with it its own challenges, as well as its own methods and practices. The most popular kind of performance writer these days is probably the stand-up comedian. In previous eras, many comedians, or comics as they were known, tended to use other people's material in bulk as their act would be comprised of a long series of quick-fire gags and one-liners. And, while this is still true today, audiences now expect a comedian to base their act on their own life to a large extent, and so material – whether written by the artist or by outside writers – is of a more personal nature. And with the necessity of television, DVD and online appearances, material is eaten up speedily and comedians are compelled to write more and more. It's a different world to that of most writers, but it can be a rewarding one.

Iszi Lawrence is a stand-up comedian who also presents a regular podcast and live show called *The Z List Dead List*. She also does a lot of ju-jitsu. We met in a café in Brighton while she had a few hours to kill before a show.

DAVID: When people think of different kinds of writer, they often tend to leave out stand-up comedians. Why do you think that might be?

ISZI: I don't know if stand-up counts as writing. You do the thinking and the looking out the window but you don't actually – well I don't – do a full script, so you don't actually type it all up. If you look at my notebooks, it's spider diagrams, mainly ideas and that sort of thing. I have the ideas in my head until I get an audience and I have the pressure of trying to push them out my face, that's where the writing happens – a lot of it is live onstage. I repeat the routines, but if I start reciting, I'm not funny at all. I have to talk to the person in front of me. It's one of those things where if I go on and I say to myself, 'I've got to do this and I've got to do that', I'm really quite awful. Where if I'm talking to a human, I tend to do quite well.

The writing process for me is coming up with the idea that's funny, keeping that in my head, and working out various ways to make it funny in my head. I'm trying to write a joke at the moment which isn't going anywhere and the only idea I've got for it is, 'What happens to that bit of plastic on the airbag on the dashboard?' 'Cos in my head what happens is the airbag smashes that piece of plastic into your face as fast as possible. How do I get that into some sort of way of the audience finding that funny?

DAVID: And how do you develop that quite slight idea into a routine? What is your usual method of doing that?

ISZI: There are various possibilities: do you frame it in a story about people, do you frame it in a story about something else? I have a similar joke which is about the anti-smoking advertisement for cigarettes. I get into it by saying that I used to smoke, and then I point out that there's no point in giving up smoking because on my last pack of cigarettes there was a picture of a pair of lungs, a horrible dead smoker's lungs, and next to that a pair of big healthy fluffy lungs. You can't help but notice that both of those people are dead, so what difference can it make? There'll be a similar route to the airbag routine but I haven't decided the best way yet.

I find in stand-up it works really well to make everything personal. The more you can make it about you, the more the audience will pay attention to you.

DAVID: So you work ideas out in your head and practise them and then do the routines on stage – do you actually have to write it down at any point?

ISZI: Yes, you do have to write it. In my last year of A–levels, I worked with Steve Best and Noel James, two very good joke writers, who were taking a sketch show to the Fringe. And the way Noel James writes his jokes is he has five minute chunks that kind of fit together and then he'll split the set around the five minutes. I've seen him do a forty minute headline set with a half hour encore and a ten minute encore after the encore, which was an hour twenty of just puns… One of my favourites of his is, 'I went on a specialist package holiday and the IRA were there. Not the Real IRA, the Surreal IRA. And they planted a fish under my car and it went off.'

I do write a lot of one-liners as well 'cos I like them, but I use my one-liners as a sort of punishment. So if they're not laughing enough, I tell them bad jokes as a way of engaging – a way of bullying them really.

DAVID: As a stand-up, you work at night and spend an awful lot of time travelling, but most people I talk to have an ordered day, so let's pretend your life is normal. When do you wake up?

ISZI: Normally I wake up between eight thirty and nine thirty, at some sort of time around then. Occasionally you wake up in a hotel room in Teesside, so you're kind of like, 'OK, what's happening?' You've got to locate yourself on the planet, you go, 'OK. I'm here, I know what's happening.' Either you're saying, 'It's Newcastle I've got to run downstairs and get some breakfast before they shut,' because it's a horrible thing for comedians that they always shut breakfast at nine o'clock because they're evil. If it's Plymouth you're thinking, 'It's raining, shall I go for a walk before going to the theatre?' That sort of thing. But if I'm at home, usually I try and get all of the admin done by midday, all the invoices I've got to send, all the gig lists, all the stuff from my agent.

DAVID: What sort of admin does a stand-up comedian have to do?

ISZI: Weirdly, a lot of my admin is Facebook. I get a lot of gig offers through Facebook and a lot of people think that's a cool way to approach it. The people with real money tend to look at my website and send my agent an email and she deals with that. Whereas I get people posting me things like, 'Hey, Tuesday night I'm sort of like starting up this new club and I was wondering are you free?' So it's that sort of thing and occasionally I'll have other work as well, like I'll have to do a poster but it's mainly things like working out the route I've got to drive, going on Google

Maps and working out where all the traffic is, working out the best… God it's boring.

So that's my mornings. Then I usually go for a run, get out and try and get some oxygen in my head. I usually eat lunch between three and four and then either I'm sitting down writing stuff for a couple of hours then going to a gig, or if it's a gig far away, I'm getting into the car and shooting off immediately. So my writing time is actually largely after shows. It's either onstage during the show or it's when I get back and I've still got the adrenaline and I'm driving in the car. The time where my brain kicks in is between eleven and two, that's when a large amount of work tends to happen, in terms of creativity anyway.

DAVID: How do you come up with material at a time of night when most of us are either asleep or drunk?

ISZI: It's very easy late at night, very easy. Then or when I go for my run or walk, because I find that getting myself as far away from a pencil as possible is basically when new ideas come to you. I don't do well if I've been inside all day, I go a bit stir crazy. I need exercise and I need to do something else.

DAVID: How much writing would you say that you do?

ISZI: Unlike fiction writers, I don't have a word count per day. You have to write for Edinburgh, which is a huge thing that acts have to go through every year. The idea is that you have fifty minutes of new material every year that's good, and then you go up to Edinburgh and lose all your money. I've semi-avoided that because I did it in 2012 and it went as well as it could possibly go. I wrote the show, went up there, got pretty good reviews, sold out a few nights and made twenty-six pounds in a month… So I tend to think, well, if everybody's up there shouting for attention, I can shout for attention down here. Which is why I got into podcasting. My *Z List Dead List* is a little project I've got about obscure people of history – I've realized that I'm not going to go down in history at all and so who are the other people who haven't? People who don't fit the great narratives. And that's been running now for a year and a half and been going well, and I've been doing my podcast since September last year and that's been going well too. Writing for that, I do have to sit down and read… I then try and find alternative sources, I don't just want to read Wikipedia.

DAVID: There's a whole generation who do all their research on Wikipedia.

ISZI: It's fine so long as you follow up and check the links. But really the podcast isn't so much about history, it's self-help, it's 'This is how these people live their lives, how do you live your life?'

DAVID: As a stand-up, your deadlines are geographical. You have to work 'where' as well as 'when'.

ISZI: Yes deadlines are very much geographical, but on the other hand, the beauty of stand-up is that really no one cares, so you can do exactly the same set in Bristol as you did in Birmingham.

DAVID: One thing that fascinates me about comedy performance and comedy writing is that often material which sounds overly written doesn't work live. Similarly and conversely, comics like Frankie Howerd never said anything that looked funny written down.

ISZI: Stand-up is a conversation much more than any other form of performance. It really is about that engagement and you can feel it when that happens. And when it doesn't happen, you're up there scrabbling. And it has to be a mutual thing as well. If there's a good heckle it saves you. If there's a bad heckle it kills you. But normally if there's a good heckle it can just flip the whole gig over and it's like, 'Oh you're back onside because that person's given me permission to be the comedian again'. And then boom! It's lovely. Whereas that doesn't happen in theatre, there's no point where the audience can't save the day. It's very rare, I hasten to add. Don't heckle.

DAVID: What's a good heckle?

ISZI: Well, it can be something really pedantic. It can be, 'That's incorrect because of this.' It's always something that's of the moment, and that's when it's good. The best heckle I've heard was a comedian called Ted who had cerebral palsy. We were at this comedy night in Cardiff in a Hawaiian bar that serves Korean food... imagine. A packed-out room and the opening spot was on and he was really right wing. He was having a go at immigration and he was really bad, he was showing off about how much he earned and how people on welfare were horrible. It just didn't fit at all and it wasn't well written or funny. Anyway. So he thinks this isn't working, I've got to engage with the audience, and he starts asking the audience questions. The questions he asks are like, 'Hey anybody got a car? Who here's got a car? I've got a car. What car do you drive? You don't have a car? Somebody in here must have a car!' At which point Ted shouts from the back, 'MOBILITY SCOOTER!'

And the laughter was huge, but it killed the comedian dead because there was no way you could respond to that. It was beautiful.

DAVID: I submit to the excellence of that heckle. One area where stand-ups differ from some other writers – not including the desire to be seen – is that they need an extra layer of determination. A writer doesn't need to show anyone their work. A stand-up has to.

ISZI: There are people who write stand-up that doesn't go anywhere, I assure you. I was backstage with a load of improv people and there was a bit in the script that said, 'Well, that didn't get a laugh' – in the script they were berating the audience for not laughing. It was interesting.

But the first stand-up I was writing was at school and I've never performed that because it was awful and I could tell it was awful. I did a gig when I was seventeen for my mate and there's a joke I should have used from it, which is awful – 'I do not talk about women's issues, period.' There is a lot of stuff that never gets put onstage.

DAVID: Do you have an accountant?

ISZI: Nope, I do all that myself. That's a nightmare. I keep receipts diligently. The good thing is my expenses are so high because of my travel, so my earnings look much less than they actually are. There is a big crisis in the comedy circuit at the moment in that fees have not gone up in about sixteen or seventeen years, and the cost of transport has. Very few clubs pay expenses. Ten years ago there were about thirty touring comedians, maybe twenty. Now there's over two hundred. And people have got less to spend on entertainment, money's tight. This is why I've got into podcasting in a big way, it's why I'm expanding my repertoire and doing the history stuff. There's a financial motivation for it as well. It's not just me going, 'Oh, that'll be fun.'

DAVID: If someone wants to become a stand-up, what specific advice would you give them?

ISZI: It's about self-knowledge really. I'd have a look at yourself in the mirror and see what an audience would see, someone who's never met you before, and start from that. Even if you think you don't look like who you are, there's an interesting thing. Mainly the thing that you would never want to say onstage in front of anybody ever is the thing that works. The confession.

You can get away with a lot if you're interesting. If you're doing a routine where, for example, you're doing a belly dance 'cos you're a fat bloke – OK, that might work for a little bit but you'll start to hate yourself and it won't get you gigs. It will get you gigs in a few places where they'll know you're a guaranteed laugh for that, but you won't progress. What you really need to do is analyse the things about you, why you want to say things, why you don't want to say things and then use that. Focus in on things that you find interesting, because I guarantee you that being interesting is key to getting attention and once you've got attention it's easy to get laughs. Once you've got an idea of a routine, it's mainly down to editing, getting rid of any unnecessary bits. If there's a bit where you say, 'That happened on a Friday and actually the rest of the story happened on a Saturday' – well, guess what? It can all happen on a Saturday. You can bend the truth a bit in order to get to the punchline faster. It's about editing everything, sprinting it down. Which is really annoying 'cos you think, 'I've got to do ten minutes tonight and I've only got ten minutes, and if I edit everything out I've only got five minutes'. But you've actually got seven minutes 'cos they're going to be laughing harder.

Also go to see a lot of comedy. Go to a lot of shows and sit in the back and think, 'OK, what's the trick here? What's actually going on? Is this person being as funny as everybody seems to think they're being? Or are they just being really boring? Doing a really obvious routine?'

It's about things that make you an individual – your stories, things that make you laugh, which includes writing puns, and the very specific way that you write. The voice that you write with takes a hell of a lot of time to find. It's your unique selling point and it's the thing that audiences will applaud. Or hate. That's the thing, it's never good to have an entire room of people who absolutely love you, because that means you're kind of boring. If you've got half the room with the people in hysterics, crying, and the other half of the room bemused and giggling and not really sure what's going on, and a couple of people just dead cross, that is the ideal thing. Then you know that the people who are crying with laughter, they're going to tell friends about you, they're going to find out about you, they're going to follow you for ages.

DAVID: What is your definition of success?

ISZI: There's no obvious stamp. There's no black belt that you can work towards. There's no big degree at the end where you can say, 'Hey, I've made it' – which is lovely in a way because once you lose that thing of 'I must be successful' and you realize that everyone has different terms of what success is and what they want… It's the avoidance of a day job that is exciting. I've managed to avoid that since 2010! I've kept two cats alive! This is amazing. I'm so happy.

And off Iszi goes, to prepare for her show, to confess the things she would never confess, and to make people laugh.

CHAPTER TEN

JASON HAZELEY AND JOEL MORRIS
– 'We Like To Take The Piss Out Of Things That Already Exist'

The classic model of a British comedy writing machine is the duo – Galton and Simpson, Clement and La Frenais, Esmonde and Larbey. These days, there are fewer writing duos, perhaps because most of them are either also performers, or writers find it financially more pleasing to work alone. But one of my favourite writing partnerships is that of Jason Hazeley and Joel Morris. Their work is both intelligent and surreal; from the extraordinary long-running local paper parody *The Framley Examiner* (please Google it, you will snort air bubbles from your brain) to their biggest hit, the million-selling updated-for-grown-ups new series of Ladybird Books (*The Ladybird Book of The Hangover, How It Works: The Husband*). Joel and Jason are brilliantly funny writers. Unusually for a writing duo, they get on really well, and have done since they were at school together. I've known them for a long time – they wrote a bit for my massively-unsuccessful Radio Four hit *Broken Arts* and, more popularly, we did a day together on the *Paddington* movie – and they are good company.

I met them in a nice pub and after some brief comedy writer nonsense, we got to it.

DAVID: You've been yoked together since the dawn of it. When exactly did you start writing together?

JOEL: We started writing together at school and we started working in comedy just after leaving school. We were taken under the wing of Barry Cryer, Peter Vincent and Ian Davidson, who wrote *Sorry* for Ronnie Corbett. We worked for Russ Abbott for a bit. And then we stopped doing that. I went to college and worked for a local paper and then we went to music (Joel was in the band Candidate, while Jason was half of Ben & Jason and now plays keyboards for Portishead on tour). We did about ten years in music before suddenly we found ourselves back doing comedy again.

JASON: Mainly because we couldn't make any money.

JOEL: I knew Charlie Brooker from way back and I did some work with him. Charlie doing his website *TV Go Home* made me think that we should do a website. Charlie said, 'It's really easy, it costs twenty-five quid, get yourself a domain name, put some comedy on it and people will see it.' And we did *The Framley Examiner* because we'd submitted some stuff to Charlie for *TV Go Home* and he said, 'This is really funny. Go and get your own fucking website.' So we did.

JASON: I think he said, 'This is very good and you know it... Piss off.'

JOEL: 'Fuck off and get your own website.' It was a different time – suddenly it was possible to do something. For twenty-five quid you could buy a domain name, put some comedy on it, point twelve people towards it and it was a small enough world back then that word would get around. We got our book deal within a fortnight of putting the website up.

JASON: It was the first time I sent an email to more than two people. I sent it to twenty-four people and said, 'You might like this.' By the end of the day, other friends of mine were sending it back to me as a recommendation, saying, 'This is brilliant, you'll like this.' And within a fortnight we had two book offers, one with Penguin and one from Random House.

JOEL: Then we cleverly went to a four person comedy writing team, and in the year we wrote *The Family Examiner*, I made £9000 and nearly starved to death.

JASON: I got £8000 cos you got an extra thousand for designing it.

DAVID: What got you writing?

JOEL: What, in the morning?

DAVID: No, generally.

JASON: It was other people's comedy. I loved it and it sounded like something achievable to me. Comedy does sound like music to me. There's a lot of rhythm and you can tell wrong notes when you hear them. My ideas were different from Joel's in that they were Monty Python, Fry & Laurie and *Absolutely!* were the three big ones. They sounded so perfect and they made you laugh.

JOEL: They seemed to be crafted, you could hear the writing. Douglas Adams was really big for me cos it sounded like he was writing. I loved Charles Schulz who did *Peanuts* – everybody knows who he is, his name's at the bottom of the cartoon but if he was in the street you'd leave him alone. I thought becoming famous would be a nightmare, you'd be bothered all the time. I'd seen the name John

Lloyd in the credits of TV shows, and thought, 'I don't know who you are but you appear to be involved with something I like.'

JASON: 'I bet you're having a shitload of fun doing this.'

JOEL: Barry Cryer or David Nobbs, these names would come up at the end of shows and you thought, 'You appear to be well-known and well-respected and no one's running after you. You don't get The Beatles crowds that come with fame but you appear to be able to do something in the arts.'

JASON: There's another impulse though. The very first thing that we ever wrote together, we were both at school, and neither of us was a sportsman – I think we were as good at sports as a man made entirely of arms probably – so instead of doing games, we spent the bulk of Wednesday afternoon in the computer room, and we used to type up the school newsletter, which was written by the headmaster with submissions from the teachers. And because we had access to the means of production, we wrote a parody one and photocopied it and sent it round a few of our mates and it got very noticed, people thought it was hilarious. So I think there was an impulse there to be naughty, to take the piss. A lot of what we do is parody because we like to take the piss out of things that already exist.

JOEL: My dad was a journalist – Jason's dad was a postman – and he had a photocopier at work. I had a typewriter, so the words looked like a newspaper if I typed it up. It wasn't just to do with it being a parody…you weren't just doing something funny, it had to look the same. Like the *Monty Python* books and the *Goodies* books. I could draw comics and my dad would photocopy them in black and white and they'd look like *Peanuts*. It would look like a newspaper so I'd hand it out with the newsletter at school.

JASON: It makes it funnier if it's the real thing but done funnier.

JOEL: We got asked when we did *Framley*, 'How do you make it look like a local newspaper?' We did it in the same software as a local newspaper.

DAVID: What's good about writing?

JASON: Here you're going to get two different opinions 'cos Jason doesn't like writing. Whereas I love it. He likes having written.

JOEL: I keep finishing and looking back at it and going, 'I have no idea where that came from.' I will do anything to avoid it.

JASON: I love it. I like getting it right. I like getting every note right and making sure that there are just the right number of notes and they're all in the right place. It feels to me like whittling really or carving, neither of which I can do.

JOEL: We both come from other artistic things like music and I was an illustrator for a bit, I used to draw a lot, and I get depressed if I go to bed and I haven't done something new. If the world contains the same number of things at bedtime as it did in the morning, I get a bit itchy. Whatever it is whether it's a drawing or a piece or music or a comedy idea or a parody ad for *Viz*, I want to do one more of those.

JASON: Sometimes there is some irritating neural compulsion where you must write this thing. I was at home yesterday doing some quite boring admin. I was feeling restless and I couldn't work out what it was – and I went, 'I know what it is, it's that blog post about *Ever Decreasing Circles* that I've been wanting to write for about three months.' I took the laptop out and it just tipped out straight away, because all those thoughts had been sitting there for three months going, 'Come on, get me out of the fridge.'

DAVID: If I'm in the shower and I have an idea for something on Twitter, I have to restrain myself from leaving the shower. What's exciting about writing as opposed to just good?

JASON: Well, there's generating something that didn't exist before. I've no fear of the blank page, I love it because it's a space for stuff. What's exciting about it? Getting it right is exciting.

JOEL: When I built railway lines as a kid and the bits didn't join up, that's what writing plot feels like to me now. Because it's so hard, I love the feeling at the end of having conquered it. There's always a lot of mountains to climb. That's the exciting thing: finding something you couldn't do and then proving that you can do it.

JASON: Yes and also – it's a difficult thing to talk about – getting a reaction. Because typically if you're a comedy writer and not a writer performer, you send in a script and then fourteen months later you'll see it go out on TV and it might have an audience laughing at it.

JOEL: …with one of your lines in it.

JASON: I once described it as a bit like putting your cock through a glory hole, getting a blowjob and then a year and a half later seeing it on the internet and going, 'Yeah I remember that. It was quite good wasn't it?'

DAVID: Something I've never experienced.

JOEL: Nor have I. But as a partnership you obviously make each other laugh and you are actually trying to top each other to some extent, so you get that laugh there. Writing comedy on your own would be a slightly odder experience I think.

DAVID: You don't laugh on your own because that would be really weird.

JOEL: But you know when it's right, don't you? You know when you've got it.

JASON: I'm still writing for approval, I think. A lot of the time you're writing for the approval of someone you don't respect, like a commissioner you've never met or the head of a studio.

DAVID: There's a thing among comedians that when someone says something funny, nobody actually laughs. They just say, 'Yeah, that's funny.'

JASON: When we started, I thought it was exactly the same as making your mates laugh in class. And what you want is the red face and the tears of laughter and someone being unable to breathe. But if you're a professional you should be laughing less and writing a bit more.

DAVID: So you get up in the morning, what are you looking forward to?

JASON: Honestly, I'm looking forward to ten o'clock when I sit down and start work. Even at the weekend I'm looking forward to ten a.m. on Monday.

JOEL: Same here.

JASON: That's a terrible thing to say 'cos I love my partner and my kids but I really look forward to working.

JOEL: Same here. We've both done other jobs and I didn't look forward to starting them. That's why I do this one, the insecure weird one. I didn't always look forward to starting work and I feel it would be ungrateful to say I don't look forward to this. I chose this.

JASON: I love my job, so I'm being paid to do something I love. Which is a bit like being Pablo Casals or the Duke of Kent, whoever he is.

JOEL: I talk to writers and the enemy is people who stop them writing. Commissioners that turn things down or people that come back and say, 'Not that, do it again and do it my way.' I tend to enjoy the beginning of the day before I've opened any documents full of notes of people telling me how to do it. I enjoy the moment before someone tells me to stop or to do it differently.

DAVID: Sitting down at the desk is a bit like getting in the cockpit if you're a pilot.

JASON: You'll notice that all my metaphors are musical. So I call the first hour of the day basically doing scales, warming up and that usually requires a bit of input, reading a bit of news, seeing what friends are up to on Facebook, joining in a bit here and there, just warming up, getting started. That's the cockpit, that's the pre-flight checks. Everything switched on. Good. 'Cos then you take off, don't you?

JOEL: I drop the kid off at school and come straight in and wait in a cafe for half an hour for the place where we work to open. That half hour I adore. I bumped into Chris Morris in a Costa and we were nattering and he said, 'I've got to go, this is my warm up time.' We were having a nice friendly chat and he says, 'Can we just stop because I've got to go away and read the paper, you've got to go away and read the paper, otherwise we're not ready for today.' We had to go and sit and read the paper on opposite sides of the café, otherwise the first phone call to come in with some orders from head office would have arrived with us unprepared for the day.

DAVID: Where do you work?

JASON: We work in two types of place. One type is an office, so if a production company has got us in for something they might give us an office. And that's usually done when you're being paid day rate stuff rather than commission stuff.

DAVID: A day rate is…?

JASON: If you're writing for TV you're paid by the broadcast minute, so someone will say to you, 'We've got a half hour programme and we'd like eight minutes of that to be stuff you've written.' So you're paid by minutes commissioned and sometimes you write more than that and sometimes they don't use it all but they have to pay you what they've commissioned you.

DAVID: How many minutes do you normally get commissioned? Working on, say, Charlie Brooker's *Screenwipe*.

JASON: That's weekly work, so we're paid a day rate. We're paid to write in the office at ten a.m. and leave at six p.m. and then between those hours we probably generate something like twelve pages of notes for Charlie and he then uses as much or as little of that as he wants.

JOEL: And the opposite to that is being paid by the minute to generate your own material, which you'll very often over generate to a ludicrous degree. You send in ten scripts and one gets considered and cut down to thirty seconds. I think more and more these days we're on day rates.

JASON: Yeah, it's taking over. It means there's no royalties attached or anything.

JOEL: The reason that Python exists is that when they were given the option of what they wanted to do after *The Frost Report* and *TW3*, Eric Idle or someone said, 'We'll never get any repeat fees if we do stuff about the news. Let's do something about nothing at all and that way it'll get repeated.' And he's been right.

JASON: So offices are one place where we work. The other place we work is in the Royal Festival Hall. It's a public building and there's a members' bar on the top floor, we're both members, and if you crash in the doors as soon as they open, you can get a seat, they've got Wi-Fi, you can buy coffee and it's got the biggest window in London so it's a fucking fabulous view. It's a lovely place to work.

DAVID: Why don't you work in each other's homes?

JOEL: Children.

JASON: Children, and an office is just too expensive.

JOEL: And other writers drop by and say hello.

DAVID: What are your quirks? Do you have music or silence?

JOEL: We put headphones on sometimes.

JASON: Obviously a lot of time we're discussing things but once we've discussed an idea, let's say it's a sketch, normally one of us comes up with the idea on the fly, makes a note, and then we chuck the idea around, find out some things that are going to be funny about it, make a note of those and then one of us will go away and write it up. So at that point where Jason is writing on his own, that's when I'll put some music on. If I need a kick up the arse, I'll listen to the 'Capricorn One' soundtrack because it's kind of telling you to get on with it.

JOEL: I listen to Jerry Goldsmith's soundtrack to *Alien*, it's the most tense thing you can listen to and it makes you go, 'God you mustn't stop writing or you'll die!'

JASON: I had to make a playlist on my phone of just instrumental stuff, stuff with no words in it, and then I could listen to that. I was getting a variety of things but I wasn't getting words.

JOEL: It's a white noise generator at least, it shuts the world out.

JASON: Our friend Toby has got a three-hour recording of rain in a rainforest that he listens to on a loop when he's writing because it just shuts out the rest of the world.

After a lengthy digression about Quentin Tarantino's musical cues, we discuss the unique nature of the writing partnership. It only really exists in comedy; with the exception of the playwrights Beaumont & Fletcher, very few dramatic writers work as duos. How does a comedy writing twosome operate?

JOEL: The cliché used to be that one of you types and one of you paces.

JASON: It was the cliché but it's also very true. Cleese & Chapman worked like that, Esmond & Larbey worked like that.

JOEL: …but most writing partnerships are under a strain because the person who's doing the typing thinks they're doing more work. We used to do that and after a while we started to do what Fry & Laurie used to do. They both wrote and would hand each other bits of paper, swapping over. It was like Consequences where you draw the head of an animal and you pass it over and somebody does the body…

DAVID: It's like the Ben Elton and Richard Curtis model, where you write a script, send it to the other person, they rewrite it, send it back to you… Moving on, what methods do you use to generate ideas?

JOEL: I think they just keep tumbling out, don't they? If it's comedy, you can pretty much write about one or two things. One is writing about an observation you've made and the other is writing about something that annoys you. If you're writing something bigger than those two, you do have to start writing about people. You start to think about who a character is, and maybe they're based on someone you've seen or someone you know. Once you're in the flow and you're working every day, the ideas just seem to tumble over themselves. It does require some input as well, you need to read things and absorb things and watch things.

JASON: If you've got a thing of some length, it's quite important to finish it, even if it's crap and even if you've got to put in placeholder lines, you should just get it done. Then you can go back to the top and start rewriting it.

DAVID: Those things you're told not to do often work really well. People are often told not to write dialogue first. I find if you've got a scene you want to work out in dialogue, then write it and come back to it later.

JASON: Also you get a pin board in your head. Someone tells you something and you just go, 'Yeah, I'm keeping that because that's going to come in useful one day.'

JOEL: We're quite good at bottom drawers. Our bottom drawer is always really full. Ideas that people didn't buy…

JASON: …or that we didn't get off the ground.

JOEL: Sometimes you go back to these things and you look back at it and think the version of it that you did wasn't good enough.

DAVID: It's like going back to a demo.

JASON: This is another writing trick that we do. What you're selling is what made you laugh in the pub. And if you've accidentally overwritten it and it's not the thing that made you laugh in the first place, then you've failed. At the very top of every sketch you have to sell the first thing that made you think it was worth writing. It's got to be the thing that first made you laugh or gasp or whatever.

DAVID: Is there such a thing as writer's block and do you carry a notepad?

JOEL: He's better at notepads than me. But Jason's handwriting is so bad that he doesn't know what any of these say.

JASON: I sometimes can't read my own notes back. I've got probably thirty or forty of these.

JOEL: Like Kevin Spacey does in *Se7en*. They're all on the wall in skin.

JASON: They're all explaining exactly how I'm going to kill again. So yeah, I carry a notebook at all times, and if I don't have one for some reason there's always the notes app on my phone here. I use the voice recorder as well. If we're walking around and we come up with a sketch idea, we'll routine a few lines of it, record them, then pause it and work out where the sketch goes next, and then record them again. So you end up with the finished script on a voice memo.

JOEL: I've just opened up my first note on here, and of course it's my idea for Village People UK. 'Who would be in the British Village People? What are the male archetypes for the British?' And the list is: 'Traffic warden, Rotarian, town cryer, park keeper, Morris man, milkman and Kwik Fit Fitter'…

JASON: You've left off 'Alderman', my favourite. There'd be an alderman in the UK Village People.

JOEL: My favourite note on here is names. Just people's names like Kirk Smeaton. I saw that on a road sign which I thought was brilliant, Toby Carvery. Andy Clockwise.

JASON: Writer's block… it does happen, it definitely does happen, I've had it a few times. Once I had it, and I approached you and Caitlin Moran and said, 'How do you deal with writer's block?' And you both gave pretty much the same answer, which was write yourself out of it. Sometimes if we're running on fumes we'll do a completely meaningless comedy exercise, like writing silly notes. We spent one entire afternoon just making anagrams of the name Dennis Potter.

JOEL: We were on a deadline, we had an eight episode series for MTV and they pulled one of the scripts at the last minute and went, 'you've got one day to write a script from scratch.' And while we were writing I tore up the letters of the name 'Dennis Potter' and we spent the entire day rearranging them and got the script done. We put a sign on the door that read: DENNIS POTTER ANAGRAM PROJECT – DO NOT DISTURB. And we spent the day with two parts of our brains running. One was doing TEN TON SPIDER and SPIDER POINTS and the other part was tricking our brains into thinking...

DAVID: How do you get work? How do you sell ideas? Do you have an agent and what is your agent for?

JASON: To begin with, it was a very steady process of being in the right pubs. It was literally that. There was an evening when Charlie Brooker said to me, 'I'm going to the pub. Graham Linehan and some other people are going to be there.' So we went along and met some people. And gradually you find what's happening is you're getting to know all the right people. It's a very small world. You get into conversations with them and they'll say, 'I tell you what, I need something written.' And that's just got bigger. Because we're quite well-established, people know who we are so they ask for us. So our agent doesn't actually get us work. She negotiates.

JOEL: We use our agent as a way of saying we've got an agent. It's important to have an agent otherwise they'll go, 'Are you just a guy in your bedroom?'

DAVID: How hack-like are you? I will do almost anything.

JOEL: We will do anything.

DAVID: But why?

JOEL: I think you can afford to be choosy if you are pretty confident that your mum and dad will bail you out. We're both first generation middle class but a lot of people come from very comfortable backgrounds. The kind of people who run DJ nights but who don't really do anything.

JASON: It's prejudiced out there in London.

JOEL: It's a Paul McCartney thing rather than a John Lennon thing. I will write anything that you require me to write and I'll make it so that you can whistle it unless it's really repulsive. We've turned down a couple of things that we thought were morally repugnant.

JASON: You try to please yourself to the extent that you try to do the job to your satisfaction. We ghost-wrote the two *Mrs Brown's Boys* books and obviously that's not our character and we're not Irish... But once we'd immersed ourselves in the character and started writing, we were trying to do the best job that we could. We channelled our mums. The first of those *Mrs Brown's Boys* books – I've said this and I'm not joking – is the most autobiographical thing I'll ever write.

JOEL: Someone said: no matter how cynically you try and write something, you've got to find what you love in it. Otherwise you'll do it badly. People think you can cynically write a rip off of *The Da Vinci Code*. *The Da Vinci Code* is the best book Dan Brown has ever read. *Harry Potter* is the thing JK Rowling loves most in the world, there's nothing cynical about it. And weirdly Brendan loves *Mrs Brown's Boys*. He's incredibly uncynical, he absolutely loves that audience and loves that joke.

DAVID: What makes you doubt what you do? What makes you think you might be good? What do you want from the future? How would you justify your life to a supernatural court?

JOEL: I completely doubt it constantly. I get the black dog. I'll go, 'This is pointless' when I find it hard or I'm not getting anything through. People say, 'No you can't do this,' and then I realize that I keep being asked to do it, so either other people are idiots or I *can* do it. You think that when your own career and your bank account say you can do it, that feeling would go away but it's still there. You still think you've tricked everybody and they're going to find you out.

CHAPTER ELEVEN

MARK ELLEN
– 'Enthusiasm Is The Most Important Thing'

Mark Ellen is one of my favourite people. His career has interwoven with mine on more than one occasion. Mark and his co-genius David Hepworth founded several of the magazines I've worked for, from *Smash Hits* and *Q* to *The Word*, and Mark's rock journalism, enthusiasm for music and editorial skills are legendary. He's also very funny, as his various presenting jobs indicate. And his excellent autobiography *Rock Stars Stole My Life* is both hilarious and a superb history of British music, music journalism and culture. Oh, and he was in a band at Oxford with Tony Blair.

I meet Mark at a restaurant in Exmouth Market (the one in London, not the one in Exmouth) and within seconds of ordering some bread to dip into olive oil, we're off. Mark leads the batting:

MARK: I can talk about any kind of writing. Is it feature writing you want?

DAVID: There are two strands to the book… One is a writer's day and the other is talking about writing in general. So – you're a publisher running a magazine and you receive some unsolicited copy. What's going to be wrong with it?

MARK: I've had thirty years of writers saying to me that they'd like to write for us and I do the same thing with all of them, I say, 'You'd like to write for us? Why don't you have a look at the magazine and send me ten original ideas that you think you are qualified to write.' By that I mean, 'My specialist subject is dubstep,' rather than saying, 'I'd like to interview Ricky Gervais,' because to deserve that you have to be David Quantick who's been writing for us for years. And when you do that, when you say, 'Send me ten original ideas,' you never hear from 97% of them ever again in your life. A lot of them think that's really unfair and also think, 'I haven't read the magazine, do I have to go out and buy a copy?' I don't see why it's unreasonable to think you've got to take an interest in me if I've got to take an interest in you.

If you write to a magazine, you've got to put yourself in the state of mind of the editor and imagine how busy that editor's life is. The best way you can do that is to imagine how you can make that editor's life easier rather than more difficult. And how you can make it easier is to send original ideas that you think the magazine should be covering and that you feel that you're qualified to write. So that's how as an editor I deal with new writers, which I think is a good system.

DAVID: I'm an experienced writer in my forties or fifties. What am I going to be doing that you like and don't like?

MARK: There are two types of people, there's the ones that you cast to write or the ones who cast themselves to write for you. As an editor you think of ideas all the time. 'Who'd be the right person for that?' The other way round is using people who write for you all the time. You're reliant on them for ideas because ideas are an absolute premium. Ideas are so important. I used to come in on the Overground, a thirty-two minute journey, sixteen stops, and I'd try and write one idea per station. Get off the train with sixteen ideas, and by the time I got the bus down to *The Word* office, I'd have that whittled down to maybe seven reasonable ideas. I'd pitch them to the boys and girls in the office and maybe three of them would finish up published, or developed. And that was a really good way of doing it.

I would rely on writers coming up with ideas. The thing that gives them an incentive to see it through is it's their own idea and they came up with it. And you're going to give them credit for that, edit them sympathetically, give them enough rope and then let them get on with it.

DAVID: Occasionally I've pitched an idea, had it rejected and then seen a version of it appear in the magazine. Ideas are really hard but you can become an ideas machine, you can train yourself.

MARK: I was an editor so I tended to think that that was part of my job. About the only thing I'm any good at: I can change a plug, I can play two scales on an alto sax, and that's literally all I've got.

DAVID: You're unusual amongst writers in that as a publisher, you've not just worked on magazines, you've actually started magazines.

MARK: Starting magazines requires a huge amount of self-belief and enthusiasm. One of the great catchphrases that I've always adhered to is Tennessee Williams' 'Enthusiasm is the most important thing in the world.' I used to say that to people who came to me looking for jobs. I'd certainly look out for it. Anybody who arrived at a job interview for me, who arrived by bicycle, I nearly always felt that I should give them a job just because only really enthusiastic people ride bicycles. Very courageous people.

I was lucky because a lot of the magazines I launched had to do with a particular way of looking at the pop cultural landscape and really believing that what you could deliver was worth time and attention. And there were enough people who thought like you, who had the same aesthetic judgement, who would subscribe to it, buy it and put you in business. *Select* magazine – which had already started but I changed that – *Mojo*, *Q* and *The Word* are all collaborative things. I didn't publish stuff that was wildly derogatory. I'm not a particularly aggressive person myself but I just thought there's so much to get excited about.

People forget that it was really funny. I think there was far too much serious stuff about. We weren't really cruel about anybody. It was fond: you're a bit overblown, you're a bit ludicrous, but we love you.

DAVID: It seems like a lost world. People go on and on about how things were better for writers in the olden days…

MARK: That's not true. It's not better for writing because it's much easier to write. People ring me up all the time, usually kids of seventeen or eighteen and they're on a media studies course – which I don't madly approve of. My personal feeling is that you worked full time in the day in a bar, which is what I did when I was a kid, and at night you wrote. You taught yourself how to write. You read books and you tried to increase your vocabulary. You tried to work out who the great writers were and hopefully not slavishly do impressions of them, but try and work out how they constructed articles, what made their pieces memorable… It's an unkind thing to say but if you go and learn songwriting for three years, do you really come out at the end and be Ray Davies or Alex Turner of the Arctic Monkeys? I wrote from the age of fourteen or fifteen, I kept a diary. A lot of the diaries aren't recording what I did in my life, they're just wanting to develop my writing. I think that's a really important thing. Anyone writing, as PG Wodehouse memorably said, must go from 'Step one, the application of the seat of the pants to the chair.' It's very, very hard work, people don't realize that. They think they'll just sit there and the muse will visit them. It's not true.

I went to a *Private Eye* lunch the other day and all eleven of the people there were writing books and we all talked about writing. We didn't talk about what we were writing. Everyone in turn told me: this is what I do. I get up at seven in the morning, answer the emails, I work for an hour, have a cup of tea, I play the guitar for twenty minutes, I have sardines on toast. Everybody had their own routines and everybody said the same thing which is that you write for six and a half hours top whack then you knock it on the head, because there's no fucking point, because after six and a half hours, you look at the last paragraph you wrote and go, 'Fucking God that's not very good,' and you think, 'I'll just find the obstacle, take it out and it'll flow again.' Then you start thinking, 'Actually I'd better go back. The whole page…the chapter…the *book* is rubbish.' It's not rubbish. You turn the computer on at seven the next morning, you see the obstacle right away, you fix it, you're away.

One of the technical things about writing that everybody seems to agree on is that you write 1000 words a day, if you write more that's good, Caitlin Moran can write 7000, but you write 1000 a day and what you do is then rewrite the last 1000 and plan the next 1000.

DAVID: A lot of people would stop mid sentence, in fact a lot would say never finish a paragraph.

MARK: Very good, keep the thought going. Brilliant idea. Ian Fleming I think wrote 800 words in the morning, didn't do anything all day, just pissed about fishing or something, smoked cigars, then he came back and had a half bottle of wine and had another go in the evening. I don't recommend this by the way. It's really bad to think you can only write when you have a drink or smoke dope. I know people who do it.

DAVID: As a writer do you have to be fast?

MARK: You do, yeah. As a writer, you get rung up by *The Times* and they say, 'Can you write us 1800 words about Leonard Cohen by four o'clock?' and you look at your watch and it's ten to one. You don't really have any option apart from saying yes. By the way, another piece of advice – if somebody asks you to write a piece, say yes. Always say yes. What's the worst that can happen? You'll learn something. You'll learn to write.

I wrote anything when I was a kid. I wrote travel brochures – Greece is the word! I wrote absolutely everything. Entire wine lists, restaurant menus, anything. Somebody asked me to do something I'd do it, just learn how to use words.

DAVID: We have that in common. I've written awards speeches, wedding speeches…

MARK: I've edited speeches for Tony Blair. It's very interesting. Because he doesn't have time to write a speech, you'd write a speech for him and he would then use bits of it and improvise other bits of it to make his own. It was very exciting to watch him talking on television.

DAVID: When I worked on *The Thick Of It* and *Veep* I was struck by how the fictional speeches weren't that different to the real thing. What goes in a political speech?

MARK: They weren't political speeches, they were speeches for music award ceremonies, like the Brit awards or the Q awards.

DAVID: I remember those, they sounded really personal.

MARK: Because he put in loads of stuff about Mountain's Nantucket Sleighride… I wrote the basic bones of what the point of the speech ought to be, and he would use some of it. I wrote Jonathan Ross's first Elle Awards speech. He knocked off my beginning and end and put in a topical joke but he used every single thing I wrote. I can remember some of the really weak gags – 'A man whose diary has less windows than Alcatraz,' that kind of stuff. Everyone was laughing at Jonathan Ross and I was thinking, 'Me! I wrote this.'

DAVID: Adaptability is the key thing here. If you can write a speech for Tony Blair or Jonathan Ross, you can write a teenage pop magazine or a rock magazine for old men.

MARK: I didn't find that at all difficult, not remotely. I was in Australia doing lectures and workshops about publishing and there was one magazine we worked on which was for survivors of the First and Second World Wars and there was one called *Barbie* for six-year-old girls. I found no problem with working on both. Because they involved exactly the same disciplines and logic that you apply to any magazine. Who are the readers? What are they really interested in? Are you addressing all of those interests? And shouldn't all of those interests be represented in every topic? Once you've got that flatplanned in a magazine you're laughing. Adaptability, absolutely.

The conversation moves on and we talk about, not the concept of the writer's day, which really does seem to have fallen by the wayside like a burly drunk at Christmas, but our old employer, the formerly aggressive and magnificently splenetic New Musical Express.

MARK: At the *NME* I got my pants in the most massive twist about what I should and shouldn't do, because the *NME* made me feel like that. Everybody was so fabulous and I was the least fabulous person in there. But I was the hardest working.

DAVID: A lot of what you did as a publisher – founding the insanely cheerful *Smash Hits* and the generally pro-everything *Q* magazine – was a reaction against the *NME's* strong negativity.

MARK: The *NME's* whole world was that there was no right answer. Even your favourite group at the time weren't safe. 'Oh there's something wrong with Joy Division! They've never read Kierkegaard! They're not Marxists!' Whereas at *Smash Hits*, we were doing completely the opposite. We had a series of questions to which there was no wrong answer. 'What colour is Tuesday? Have you ever been sick in a gum boot? Does your mother play golf? Have you ever felt like a roundabout?' Those are brilliant questions, they're open questions, there's no wrong answers, and they lead to revelations. You'd have someone like Robert Smith from The Cure saying, 'Well, when I was a kid I used to have this recurring dream…' Robert Smith. Already we're away, we've got some insight into who you are. Very interesting.

DAVID: If you were starting a publication now, what would it be and what would it contain and where would it be?

MARK: I don't know if I can answer that.

DAVID: What would you not do?

MARK: I wouldn't make it mainstream. It would be specialist. It's a difficult question to answer. There are areas in publishing that suit print media. One of those is fashion, and there's a very obvious reason for that: fashion is a very tactile thing, it's about image mongering, it's about beautiful images. And the beautiful images you see in a fashion magazine printed on the page are infinitely more stunning than they would be if they were shot online. Also fashion is about positioning. There's two types of advertising. There's advertising that tells you that David Quantick's band has an album out on Tuesday and this is where you can buy it. And then there's a type of advertising that says David Quantick's formed a fragrance franchise and paints an incredible picture of the Nevada desert with Joshua trees and strange animals and beautiful women in bikinis. And that creates the concept of what David Quantick's cologne is going to smell like. Those things only work on paper.

There was a conversation at the end of *Word* magazine, which was, 'why don't we double the price of the magazine?' It was a fiver. Why don't we just double it and if more than half the people stay with us, that's great. It's great for them because they think it's worth £10 and it's great for us because we make more money and we can stay in business. I thought that was a really interesting way of looking at things because people will pay an enormous amount for things they really, really want.

DAVID: Is it harder to be a writer now?

MARK: No it's not harder to be a writer. It's infinitely easier. It's much harder to be a *good* writer. People ring me up and say: I want to be a music journalist. I don't know how I feel about being asked that as I'm not sure if being a music journalist as a career is still an option. But I don't know. I understand what they're trying to say. My advice to them is: publish yourself. When I started there were only four outlets for this stuff – *Record Mirror*, *Sounds*, *Melody Maker*, *NME*. One of the reasons they were so good was because it was so hard to get into them as a writer.

I went out for a beer with a nineteen-year-old student. It was fabulous. He had written a marvellous piece on his blog, a 5000 word appreciation of a record that only you and I have ever heard of, 'In The Court Of The Crimson King' by King Crimson. But it had no headline, it was just a kind of mind splurge, just a load of thoughts about what he thought of this record, so it wasn't journalism. So I said to him: the next time you write, why don't you work out if it should have a trajectory? This is the best record ever made, this is the worst record ever made, this is the most influential record or this is the most fascinating record ever made. That would give it some sort of shape and you can follow that particular arc and do all the things you should do in journalism: start out with your proposition, you evaluate it and you scrutinize it and you add loads of information and you modify it and in the end you come to a conclusion. I think good journalism ought to help people form an opinion.

DAVID: There's a fine line between opinion and hectoring.

MARK: The hectoring columns are there just to wind people up, to compare or contrast their opinions with, to either agree with or feel smug and self-satisfied that they were right in thinking what they thought in the first place. A writer they really like agrees with them, a writer they really hate disagrees with them. It makes them feel good.

DAVID: Can you give me some journalistic essentials?

MARK: You cannot over emphasize how difficult it is to get going. If you can't get a great first paragraph, no one's gonna read it. I always thought that there were about six ways to start a piece. One is just purely a description, *Guardian* sports writers do this all the time, they start their pieces on the Monday reviewing Saturday's game. They always start, 'With his head in his hands, a vein pumping in his temple like a drain pump… He knew where it had gone wrong.' So right away you're in the dressing room.

Then there's the brilliant quote. I can still remember brilliant quotes. 'Keith Richards doesn't so much burn the candle at both ends as apply a blow torch to the middle.' I still remember that as an opening to a piece in *The Sunday Telegraph*.

Statement of fact. You write, 'One in three babies born today will live to be 100,' you've got people's attention.

Questions are good. And the question trip which is when you've got a trip at the end of it: 'Sam boarded the private Learjet at 8:15, occupied his usual seat, feasted on salmon and had a glass of milk.' And then you discover this is Johnny Depp's dog? Johnny Depp had a dog that was flown out of New Zealand recently in a Learjet. These little twists.

DAVID: The bad way to start is with 'I was…'

MARK: Avoiding clichés… 'A posh hotel.' All hotels are broadly posh. 'We visited their ancient stately home on a sunny afternoon,' would be better as 'the watery sunlight filtered through the leaded casebook window of…' A lot of writers just don't make the effort to come up with decent work and to make it memorable. I still have a file I started twenty years ago called Top Phrases – Top must have been a contemporary word – I still use it. I use it all the time. I find a phrase I like, I put it in there.

If you're writing about people – and it's a real skill, it took me a while to figure it out – is that you've got to come up with something original about them and it helps to try and identify the one thing they do that's unique. Bob Dylan, for example, tends to sign autographs with his left hand but he's right handed. I interviewed Richard Wilson once, the actor comedian, and he referred to cocaine as 'boosty woosty.' Just writing that Richard Wilson refers to cocaine as boosty woosty, already you've learned something absolutely unique and fabulous about him. Julian Cope has a dog called Iggy Pup. Once you know he has a dog called Iggy Pup and he calls his wife Ur Indoors, you've kind of got a handle on Julian Cope.

When people went out on interviews for *Word*, I used to ask them how it went? And they'd say, 'Jane Fonda, amazing, she said this about politics and the environment and she said this about her brother.' And you think, 'I've heard all this, it's what she said to the *Evening Standard* about twenty years ago and to *Elle* magazine ten minutes after you left the room.' So I would say – find your own peg, your own vision of what happened. What was she wearing? What were her mannerisms? What did she look like? Did she have a gang with her? How did she talk to them? Did her telephone suddenly go off? Did she take the call? Who was it and what did she say? Did she have any kind of perfume? Smoke any cigarettes? How did she smoke them?

There are incredible amounts of information that you can derive from the briefest split second. But you've got to be looking for it.

DAVID: My technique is always to let people talk.

MARK: You ask short questions. And you're not embarrassed to go: in what way? There are certain questions that are brilliant and 'in what way?' is one. There are times when people say something that threatens to be interesting but it hasn't got enough detail. People you're talking to don't have a journalistic head and they don't value what they're saying. You have to go backwards and ask them to retell that story until you finally get to the nugget of that story.

DAVID: I think you're the only person in this book who's written their memoirs. What are the techniques of the autobiographer?

MARK: You cannot put in a story unless it makes a point. Otherwise you're just telling a series of fast-fading after-dinner anecdotes. They all have to be related to the central theme which is the point I'm making about pop music. What interesting and hopefully explosive celebrity-based story will make that point? I'm not just telling a story for the sake of telling a story.

In my book there's only one story that has no point, which is a story about me going to a dinner and finding that I'm sitting next to the – quite militantly – vegetarian rock star Chrissie Hynde and I've ordered the pate de fois gras and the rack of lamb.

DAVID: A comedy of embarrassment.

MARK: The next day I got to the office and everyone said, How did it go?' I said, 'Really, really badly, it was a shit evening.' I hadn't been able to sit outside of the situation and see it as a really good story. I told my colleague Kate Mossman who thought it was really funny. The next week we did our podcast, and I tried it out on the podcast and we got a terrific reaction.

This is another interesting thing about journalism. The version of the interview that you tell your mate in the pub is often the version that works the best. 'Honestly, she was hilarious, she fell over and one of her high heels broke…' And that actually might be an unconscious editing process. You're editing it one way for a piece of journalism and another way for somebody sitting in the pub. And it's often someone sitting in the pub that's getting the best version of that story.

And that's exactly how I felt talking to Mark. Experience, wit, insight and – underrated in the harsh world of writing – enthusiasm have made him what he is today. Always reading, always thinking, always up for the great quote.

Which leads us nicely into our final conversation…

CAITLIN MORAN
– 'Write The Weird Stuff, Write The Shameful Stuff'

And so we sit back, on either our bare floorboards in a room illuminated by the candles of despair or, if we are feeling good about ourselves for once, our laurels. Writing is, like so many things, very often its own reward. It's hard to do, except when it isn't, and frequently it's no fun. But that's all right, because it's probably no fun carving a giant eagle but at the end of all that hard work and broken nails, wow! You've got a giant eagle.

I don't have a giant eagle to end this book with, but I do have the next best thing. Caitlin Moran is a novelist, columnist, and sitcom-writer. She's best known for the astonishingly good *How to Be a Woman*, which is a cross between a feminist manifesto and a mammoth gush of foaming brilliance, but as a writer she is more accomplished than a successful mission. I met her when she was a seventeen-year-old force of nature on a TV pop show and over the years I have watched her became even more forceful, a success in a world which doesn't always like outspoken, intelligent funny women.

As it's the last chapter in the book, and we have to maintain some connection to the original concept of A Day In A Writer's Life, I met Caitlin in a nice club where we had our dinner and I conducted what can only loosely be called an interview. For large stretches of the interview, I was able to interject so rarely that I could easily have nipped out, learned to drive a tank and come back later on. Caitlin talks as she writes, which is brilliantly, and left me two choices when it came to editing this conversation – insert lots of whatever the verbal equivalent of a television interview 'noddy' is, to show that I was listening, or just let the tide of brilliance flow unstemmed. In the interests of truth and not exploding from trying to intervene in my own book, I have gone largely with the latter.

We begin our conversation by mocking the menu (it seems to have been assembled by a Random Dinner Generator) and then discussing the nature of the book and how its contributors fall into a variety of categories as writers...

CAITLIN: So what category am I? Basically, there's a million things I can talk about. Like column writers who are different from book writers, who are different from novel writers, who are different from TV, who are different from film, who are different from stand-up...

DAVID: You've certainly done a lot of different things.

CAITLIN: Am I a polymath then? Am I protean? I used the word 'protean' without knowing quite what it meant, but it's just been in my mind recently. The three revelations I've had about writing were, one, I always wanted to be a writer from a very, very early age, thinking I should write, not even questioning it, just thinking that I will write. I wrote my diaries at the time as if I believed an audience would read them at some point in the future – to the extent where I dedicated the first one to Judy Garland. At the beginning it goes, 'This diary is dedicated to Judy Garland.' The second one is dedicated to Debbie Reynolds. And the third one is dedicated to a Hollywood minor player, so minor that no one has ever heard of him, Oscar Levant, he was in a couple of musicals and was just incredibly funny. By that time I had read Groucho Marx's biography and knew that he was one of the Algonquin Round Table. So I'd always knew I was going to be a writer.

DAVID: Can I just ask a question here?

CAITLIN: Oh you don't need to, I self-interview. I'll literally pick subjects out of the sky. If at any point you think this is not what I wanted, do say. And so I did become a writer. I started writing a novel at thirteen that was published when I was sixteen, which was based on what my family was like, then I started working for *Melody Maker* when I was sixteen, and I got that job by the simple expedient of sending them some work. Basically I was reading this piece by Keith Waterhouse where he was explaining that he became a columnist and he read all the newspapers, decided which one he wanted to work for, decided what kind of column he'd want to write and what page it was on, worked out what would be the best column to have on that page given everything else they had in the paper, where the gap in the market was and then every day for a week sent perfect column to the editor of that section going, 'this is the column I would have written for you today if you had employed me.' And literally at the end of it they gave him a job, so I was like OK, I hear you. Is that not a great story?

DAVID: I was thinking of Keith Waterhouse before you mentioned him because he wrote a book, posthumously printed, called *How to Live to Be 22*, when he was twenty-two, all about being twenty-two.

CAITLIN: That's fucking brilliant. I would so love to read that. That's the thing you realize later – so much of what I do as a writer is tell other people how they can be a writer too, like leave a trail of breadcrumbs, well not even a trail of breadcrumbs because that's just too obscure. To literally tell people how to do it because there's two kinds of writers, the kind who draw the drawbridge up and try and make themselves look fantastic and they use their words to make themselves seem unapproachable and to stop criticism, and the ones who share ideas and make other people think they can join in a conversation with you. And it's the difference between someone preaching at you from a stage in a cape with a spotlight on them and smoke and mirrors going everywhere, which tends to be the ones that you love when you're a teenager because you love that impressive shit, you're very easily bamboozled.

DAVID: There is a feeling among some people that to be a writer you have to be some kind of mysterious intellectual. There's nothing wrong with mysterious intellectuals, but they are, as you say, not encouraging role models.

CAITLIN: The thing is I always steered clear of them. When I joined *Melody Maker*, everyone was talking about French existentialists. They were all, 'Have you read Baudelaire? Have you read Camus? Have you read *On the Road*?' and I was like, 'Well, I gave them a go for a bit but they were really low on ROFL.' Even then I was, 'I don't think I'd want to hang out with those people. They're not writing to be my mates, they're writing to either overawe me or fuck me.' You may want to look up at something and that's OK, but if you want to be a writer, you want to look for the writers that feel like they're standing next to you and going, 'OK we're going to talk about something now.'

DAVID: Which writers might these be in your case?

CAITLIN: All the ones that are seen as very lowbrow usually. Clive James, Douglas Adams – when I was thirteen, Terry Pratchett was incredibly influential to me. I was reading loads of nineteenth-century literature as well and I loved *Jane Eyre* and the Brontes and all that shit, did my Tolstoy time and all that kind of stuff, but Douglas Adams was a key one for me, he was such a humanitarian, he was a geek twenty-years before it would get you laid, he was interested in ideas. He was basically inventing the future. I was reading *The Hitchhiker's Guide to the Galaxy* and thinking, 'Wouldn't it be incredible if you had this thing that you could hold in your hand that was an electronic guide that could tell you everything about the world when you wanted to know about it?' or 'What if you did have a device that translated things for you?' With the Babel fish and the Guide he invents the iPhone and Google Translate.

So that's what I like, I'm happy to not be super cool, I want to be friendly and informative and I want people to feel good about humanity. I want to share ideas. I want to feel that I can formulate the future a bit, rather than just reporting on what's happening or moaning about what happened. I'm interested in forming a cheerful and lovely and amusing future. So now you may ask me your first question.

DAVID: Let's talk about the gap between what you do now and when you were sixteen you were writing reviews of Crazyhead and similar bands of the late 1980s.

CAITLIN: They were very interesting years – and soon to be dramatized in the film *How To Build A Girl* on Film

4 – but that was one of the big lessons of my life. You've got to remember that before the internet there were very few places you could get your information, so if you read the music press as a whole – *Melody Maker, NME, Select* – pop stars talking about things was often the only way that you could get information. They would talk about philosophers, they would be talking about Guy Debord and you'd go, 'Oh wow, he sounds like a hip and happening cat, let's go and find out about that,' then you'd go and get a book and read about it. They were avatars.

When I was writing *How To Build a Girl*, I wanted to invent a pop star that gave credit to that educational process that you had in those days and how important pop stars were as kind of an educational process. Whenever I've seen a rock star in a film, he's always some coked-up sort of black-leather-clad fucknut: he doesn't care about anything, he's just about girls and posing. Those weren't the rock stars that I loved, particularly in the era that I came out of, late Eighties, early Nineties. You'd have the Jesus & Mary Chain talking about all these bands, you'd have My Bloody Valentine there or Teenage Fanclub just being fantastic conversationalists down the pub, or the Manic Street Preachers blowing your mind. And they were all generally working-class Celtic boys who would sit down the pub with a packet of Silk Cut – as Richey Edwards said, 'They're the working-class women's cigarette and I smoke them in solidarity' – and you'd all be in your leopard skin and you'd be sitting there talking about literature for five hours.

I was a sixteen-year-old girl and these boys were only five or six years older than me but seemed so much older. We'd all be out and they would tell you things, there would be this gateway into this Narnia of information and sub culture and I was a weird fat girl realising there was a third option which was you can be ugly or you can be pretty – that's generally what society told you – and the third option was you could go weird. So I loved this world and it was incredible to enter into it, but the way that it was written about – as I found out when I joined *MM* – was the absolute antithesis of everything I believed. It was such a negative place. You weren't allowed to talk about bands that you loved, there was this arms race of snarkiness…

At the beginning I was like OK, I'm here to prove myself and if the boys' game is snarkiness that's how I will prove myself. So I just became cuntier and cuntier until I ended up peaking with a review of Ned's Atomic Dustbin where I wished them dead, I pretended I was giving the eulogy at their funeral and I was throwing the earth onto the singer's face and talking about how they were horrible squeaky unfuckable virgins. I had to look at that review two years ago when I was writing *How To Build A Girl* and I could not read to the end of this review. I had to bite down on a wooden spoon and go to the end of the garden and literally couldn't bear to read what I had written, and that was twenty-two-years later. Evil, absolute evil, and my reign of evil finally came to an end when the man who in the future was to become my husband, who would never say critical things to anyone ever, just came to me one day and went, 'That was a bit…off.' And simply strategically using the word 'off' I suddenly just went, 'hang on…'

Some squid arrive. On plates, that is, not to join us for dinner.

DAVID: All these influences and people and ideas have gone into you at an unusually early age. How did they all come out again?

CAITLIN: I've very often likened it to a digestive process, which is exactly what you want to hear before you start eating some squid. You put loads and loads of words in and eventually you start pooping out articles and features and books and stuff if you read enough.

A huge amount of what I do now, feminism and stuff, is because I love to be able to say something that no one has said before. For an enormously long time, I would look at what existed already and think, 'I've got to be like that.' And I spent a very long time trying to be 'like that' and then I had this massive revelation when I was thirty-four – 'All of that's done, just turn your gaze to over here,' and you suddenly realize that there's literally a whole universe of stuff that hasn't been written about. It's the stuff that people are scared of, or ashamed about, but you just go to the shame and the hot place and things that you would talk about with your friends at three o'clock in the morning and write those things.

If we went into that bar next door, within an hour a woman would come up to us and she would open the conversation by telling us the first time she masturbated. I have collected more people's first wank stories than anyone else in the world. I had a woman who ran alongside a train leaving the station telling me that her and her girlfriend at school – she was about fifteen years old – had formed a wanking club and would swap techniques whenever they met every Thursday. So that was a huge one.

The abortion chapter in the book got the book banned in the Middle East but apparently they have reading parties there where people bring it and read it out loud to each other. In Catholic countries where they said they wouldn't publish the book if we had that chapter in, I made them keep it in there. When I do these signings that go on for three or four hours, you get girls literally going, 'Thank you for page 64, thank you for page 261,' and I know which pages they are because they are the ones I've never written about before. When I do these talks, I say to anyone who wants to be a writer, when you're young and you're working class or if you're of colour or if you're LGBT or if you're a woman, you spend so much time thinking that you have to write like the other people. Your key skill is writing about things that no one's ever written about. Write the weird stuff, write the shameful stuff, go right to the heart of the shameful, weird stuff and just refuse to be ashamed anymore. When you write it, you become in control of it and it becomes your story and no one can shame you about it anymore. You change the way the conversation's had about the subject.

DAVID: One day you're living at home and the next you're a writer. Is that something that just developed?

CAITLIN: There was a point where I got really angry that I hadn't won any awards. I'd never been nominated for Young Journalist of the Year even though I'd been in *The Times* since I was eighteen and it was now too late for me to be Young Journalist of the Year, I was about twenty-six. And so I sat and – you have to understand that during those years between eighteen and twenty-four, I was just very, very stoned[1]. I was smoking about two-hundred

---

1   See Appendix 3

quid's worth of weed a week and then I went mental and stopped getting stoned and started getting angry that I hadn't won any awards. And one day I just sat down and read everything I'd written for the past couple of years and it just waffled on.

And you realize that if you're writing a column it's a really simple thing. Nine times out of ten it's three parts. You've got an intro, you've got a middle section, an end. In the intro you want to come in at an angle that no one else has hit before. It's like a pool table. Everyone's got the same pool table, which is all the subjects that are available, and all the writers are circling round the pool table. Now, most writers will just line up the balls in the easiest way and go, 'Right I want to get that ball in that pocket, I'll stand here and I'll bang it in there,' and that's a straightforward column. That means – no offence – you'll be a columnist on a local paper or if you're very well connected, you'll get a column on a national paper and I'll try not to be bitter about that but there we go.

What you really want to do is walk around the table and find at least a third angle, if not a fourth angle, so in the end you're bouncing the balls off of here, here and here before you've got into the pocket. If you want to change someone's mind, you have to make sure the first 300 words – that's about what you've got – hit them right from the fucking sides. They've got no idea what you're fucking on about until right at the end of that first section, the last line of the para, where you go, 'And so this is why I'm going to be talking about this.' And that's where you can change people's minds.

In that first section – particularly working for *The Times* – I'm a raging radical lefty feminist gay-loving pinko and I'm very aware that I'm writing to retired Colonels in Surrey who genuinely will say 'harumph' if they read something they don't like. But I wanna change their minds and I'm in there writing about abortion, rape, racism and all this kind of thing. So the first part, there's no point going in and going 'This is good!' or 'this is bad!', you want to start with a beautiful analogy, you want to start with a sideways thing, and lure them into it. By the time they're halfway through the second par they have to keep reading through to the end 'cos they're confused, they don't know what's happening, but they like the ride. And ninety per cent of my energy is put into trying to change people's minds and writing in a way that doesn't make anyone angry. I don't want to make anyone angry even though I'm writing about really big things, really contentious things, I don't want anyone to throw their paper down and go 'NO!' I want to change people's minds, I want them to keep going to the end.

DAVID: It sounds to me that you prefer proper essays rather than pieces whose whole attitude is, 'I don't give a fuck what you think.'

CAITLIN: So much writing that I read is just the writers having fun. I've seen a lot of porn where people seem to enjoy wanking onto each other's faces but that's not what I would do. I want us both to be involved in this, in that half the job is the reader's. I like that compact, I think that's really beautiful, the pair of you reading together. One of the things that's very sad is you see so many young writers starting out thinking they've got to be really angry and I'm like, 'Are you angry there or are you actually a bit scared that no one's reading?'

Pretend you're talking to a friend, pretend you're talking to someone who's a bit scared, pretend you're talking to someone that's about two years younger that you want to comfort rather than someone who's three years older that you want to impress.

DAVID: Your kind of column embraces people and it's saying we're all scared. The other kind of column, it seems to me, is saying, 'Let me help you be more scared.'

CAITLIN: Yeah, I find that non-useful. I think a lot of it's from being a big sister who lived with a family that had a precarious existence. We couldn't afford to be any more scared because we were absolutely fucking terrified, we were living on benefits in Thatcher's Britain. Had we read the *Daily Mail*, we'd probably have just killed ourselves. I know how non-useful that stuff is so I don't want to increase the fear, man. Mankind's a fearful species. Fear's been around a lot longer than calm and progress and progressiveness and humanism and humour and an idea of a better future and I like these more recent inventions. I'm not so much for the primal fear and hate thing. I'm a lover not a fighter. I can love my way out of a situation.

The other thing is that I don't think I could have been a good writer really until I hit about thirty because I just hadn't done that much and I think you do need to do stuff generally – maybe that's just because I'm feral and didn't go to university and stuff – but I guess you could be a great writer if you had had this incredible education, read all these things and you could apply Greek theory to things. I can't, all I've got is good old British common sense and twenty years of getting quite pissed a lot and putting yourself in weird positions and meeting weird people and trying to do different things, and that gives you completely different angles on doing things as well, living a weird and unusual life and reading as many weird things as possible.

So I'd say to young people, 'Don't expect that you can be great before you're thirty,' and put aside half the time to go off and do really weird things, because you'll never be able to do it when you're older.

DAVID: What do you think your autobiography up until sixty will be like?

CAITLIN: *How To Build A Girl*, the last novel, is the first of a trilogy. This one's *How To Build A Girl* then it's *How To Be Famous* and the last one's *How To Change The World*. We follow the same characters all the way through thirty years.

Caitlin discusses the plots and idea of these three books, which leads me to ask how difficult it is to be yourself as a writer when you live so much of your life in the public eye. It's not an issue that all the writers in this book face, but it does reflect the conversation I had with Jon Ronson in Chapter One and for many successful writers, it's a problem for any writer who's arguably as well-known as their work.

CAITLIN: I would genuinely have to ask you how much in the public eye it feels like I am. I try and avoid everything. I won't do telly unless it's a very direct bit of promo. I get asked on *Question Time* and *Have I Got News for You* and fucking *8 Out Of 10 Cats* and *QI* and all that fucking thing. I turn everything down. I don't do any red carpet. I try not to be in the public eye at all. It actively gets in the way, anybody knowing who I am. I didn't really realize when I wrote a book and put my face on the cover of the book that would mean people would know who I was.

I think it's really important for me, not being on television, because then you just arrive in people's houses uninvited and then you just fuck them off, so I try and keep out the way as much as possible. I know when I'm going to get recognized. If there's a girl with eyeliner and really nice brogues on and a vintage dress, she will come up to me and go, 'Thanks for talking about masturbation.' Homosexuals, librarians, teachers, trade unionists, girls with eyeliner, Manic Street Preachers fans, so about thirty-five per cent of the population…

At this point in the conversation I remember that this book is supposed to be about a writer's day.

DAVID: When did you wake up?

CAITLIN: Today? Well, five cos we're doing this thing. *(Caitlin was, at the time of writing, organizing the Campaign for Syria refugee charity single 'Help Is Coming'.)* So I woke up at five, went downstairs, and we've got someone staying with us who's been helping with all the internet stuff, so we had a two hour meeting in the kitchen until seven and then the kids came down. And they're of an age where they just get themselves ready now so we made them their smoothies as I always do. I said, 'Would you like me to put avocado and spirulina in it?' and they went, 'Fuck off, just bananas.' And they went off to school. Then we had another two hours of emails and stuff. That's quite unusual because we're not usually doing a Campaign for Syria.

And then I wrote my column, which I had already thought about... Whenever I write a column, I already know what it's going to be about a week in advance. I've got lists and lists, I've got them all planned about six weeks in advance. I spend a week thinking about it so that when I have to sit down and write it takes me on a good day forty minutes, on a bad day three hours.

DAVID: How many words?

CAITLIN: 850. And then I went for a swim in order that I not go mad while I worked out what I was going to write tomorrow, I've got to get moving on the film tomorrow. Came back and spent another half an hour doing emails then came out to see you. But usually when we're not doing the Campaign for Syria, then I wake up about seven, see the kids off and I write in the exact amount of time and do all my business in the exact amount of time between them going to school and coming back. The minute they come back, I clock off and they explain to me now what boots they're buying in Topshop and tell me a very long complicated story about Hannah said something about Poppy said something about India and it was a lie because she never, she literally never. And then we go to bed. It's a very unglamorous life. I very rarely socialize.

We talk about children for a while and then, well, I'm not sure, because I've had a glass of wine at this point but we return to the main topic, I think, about now.

DAVID: Let's talk about working from home for a while.

CAITLIN: When *(Caitlin's husband)* Pete used to work at *Time Out* – and he was a writer as well, so we both had exactly the same job – he would come back and I'd go, 'How'd you do babe?' and he'd go, 'I might have done about half of that feature,' and I'd be like, 'How could you have done half a fucking feature in a day?' And he'd go, 'Well, so and so came over and wanted to talk about her boyfriend, and then someone came in and they've invented a new flavour of Kit Kats and we all had to eat that for a bit and then we went for lunch and someone wanted to get drunk and then…' and you'd just get your day fannied away. And that's just being in the office. On top of that there would be a commute.

I know I just sound like a mewling kind of grandma from the nineteenth century but every time I've tried to be in town for a meeting at nine o'clock, within two hours you just sit there going, 'This doesn't fucking work, this does not work.' I'm sweaty and useless by the time I get to work. I'm very lucky, my biggest advantage in life is that I didn't go to school, I didn't go to university and I've never worked in an office. So all I've done for the last thirty-five years of my writing life is sit on a chair completely uninterrupted, just completely doing what the fuck I want, never having to talk to anybody I don't like or put on outfits that I find unpleasant and belittling in order to get onto a crowded sweaty train and spend all day having my time pissed away by people I don't care about. If there was anything I'd say that's given me an advantage it's that.

I genuinely don't understand how anyone has ever done anything if they've ever had to leave the house or talk to people. That's what gets in the way.

Caitlin discusses her manifesto for the future, which I've edited out here as it's her manifesto and besides, I've thought of a question.

DAVID: You've strewn this conversation with pieces of advice for young writers. Do you have more advice?

CAITLIN: One, obviously, always write down any idea you have and write it down in as much detail as possible. Like today I was looking at my iPhone where I've got all my ideas and one of them is just 'glass castle'. I have literally no idea what that means, but clearly at one point I thought I could get a column out of it. The second piece of advice is that if you have to write regularly, start thinking about it a week in advance because you don't want to be thinking when you get to the table. It's like when you're writing a screenplay you need an outline, because if you're sitting down and trying to write a plot, when you get into dialogue you're fucked. You need to have the outline there and it amazes me the amount of columnists who don't know what they're going to write and they just sort of make it up when they're sitting at the table. That's terrifying.

If you tell your brain to come up with an idea for something, it usually will. There's an amazing documentary I saw a couple of years ago that drew parallels between creativity and mental illness, the way that if you're schizophrenic and you hear voices in your head, there's no real difference between that and being a novelist and hearing the characters talking in your head. For instance if I said, 'Imagine if *(writer and broadcaster)* Stuart Maconie was here now, what would he be saying if he was going to chip in on this conversation?' then we could both sit here and have a pretty good punt on what Stuart was going to say. We've got little golems of the people we know in our heads and you can create these golems to run little tasks for you. You just tell your brain – it's like I know what the outline is but I'll tell my subconscious to write it and by the time I come and sit down it will do it.

The other thing is, write as much as you can. In one way, the worst thing that ever happened to me was writing *How to Be a Woman* because it nearly killed me. At one point I was having to write 20,000 words a week minimum to hit those deadlines and do all my other stuff. But on the other hand, I must have hit some kind of velocity and I could feel another part of my brain opening up – and writing's always been incredibly easy for me ever since. It nearly fucking killed me, but it's like being an athlete, I guess. You stretch all these muscles and you tear them and it really hurts, but at the end of it you can just keep on running and, as long as you keep it ticking over, it genuinely is a piece of piss. I've never had writer's block.

DAVID: I don't think writer's block exists.

CAITLIN: Nah. I think it's when you're too scared to write. I think you always know what you want to write, I think you're just too scared to write it. The amount of times I've talked to writers and they've gone, 'I've got writer's block,' and you talk to them and they go on to say, 'I don't think I can say that.' And you're like, 'It's not writer's block, it's writer's fear.' It's not that you don't know what to say because writers deep down really always know what they want to write. You're compelled to go for the bold thing or the thing that catches your eye the most, that's what we're trying to do, we're trying to find the sparkly thing. And so we're never blocked, we're just too scared to take the prize.

DAVID: What are the things in your writing that keep turning up?

CAITLIN: I have recurrent themes. David Bowie, birds, Elizabeth Taylor, making yourself – there's a million different things I could write on the theme of making yourself, I think it's so important. Particularly for women, so much self-loathing, just not realising that if you loathe yourself, make another one. So, a million things. Anxiety a lot, mental illness a lot. Cars. The Beatles. The future. It took me a very long time to realize the world hadn't always been like that and the world will necessarily have to change in the future and so the whole game is just trying to be the one that elbows their way to the front and going, 'I'd like to have a hand in the future please,' whatever way it takes.

Writers do that in a really beautiful way. That's why I love Douglas Adams, just realising these things. It's the whole 'if you build it they will come' thing. If you're a writer you can suggest these things and if someone was to take it up who is better qualified than you and is better at paperwork and admin, then we've all done our little bit. And if I can make a couple of LOLs on the way then this time ain't been in vain.

DAVID: I would say that as a writer who works 'in the now' that you're created by the time but also outside the time as well.

CAITLIN: If I could say I had one skill, it's that I can see where there's a gap in the conversation or when the tide's about to come in again. When I learned surfing a few years ago – something that I would never have thought I'd find myself saying – I learned that there's only two skills to surfing. One is being able to get up on the surfboard and the other one is waiting for the right wave. The key thing is when you see the right wave coming from far away, you're like, 'OK, if I write about this, loads of people are going to want to talk about this. This is the wave you're going to ride into shore.' I read every newspaper and magazine and try to monitor what's going on as much as possible so you can work out what the next wave is that's coming in. That's the key thing to being a writer. Once you've learned how to pop up on your surfboard, monitor the scene like a wry old Roy Scheider character. Or Keanu Reeves in *Point Break*.

DAVID: You've written about your life in book form, in sitcom form and film form, how does that differ? Apart from writing INT. FRONT ROOM, how does it feel?

CAITLIN: Well first of all, you have no idea how much I didn't know how to write INT. FRONT ROOM. When we started writing that sitcom, my sister had written like one play before. I had no idea how to work *(script-writing program)* Final Draft.

I've had some people go, 'Hang on we've got an autobiography about you, fat working-class teenage girl who's obsessed with sex, and you've written a TV sitcom where there's a fat working-class teenage girl who's obsessed with sex and now you're writing a film that's about a fat working-class teenage girl who's obsessed with sex. Are you running out of inspiration?' No, this is literally a foregone plan. It's like a Woody Allen deal. He only ever writes about neurotic New York Jews. I will only write about fat working-class teenage girls who are obsessed with sex to the point where once I finish this trilogy the next one after that is set in the sixth century in Scotland and it's about the second wave of Christianity and the power of women in that era and that will also be about a fat working-class teenage girl who's obsessed with sex. They are key in so many ways.

Women don't know what they are yet, like if you've got any vague sense of history and patriarchy and stuff, like women have never been just allowed to be women. We were so close when we got emancipation and the vote and we're slowly working out what we are and I think we're going to end up being very different to men. But where we are at this point in our evolution is like teenage girls who are only just starting to experiment with their sexuality, still quite insecure, we kind of laugh really manically and we want to get a bit pissed and take drugs but like in ten years we'll all settle down a lot more so, teenage girls at the point where you're deciding what you're going to be, it's such key form because I think as a female species we are basically teenage girls working out what we want to be at this point. And that area's very juicy for me.

At this point, the noise of media types having their dinner sweeps up and renders the recording inaudible, only becoming clear again when Caitlin says…

CAITLIN: … a massive fucking dick, swaggering down the street in your leopard skin, misquoting *Wuthering Heights* and thinking it's about someone called Healthcliffe. A glorious knob, I love a glorious knob.

And then Caitlin asks me a question.

CAITLIN: Did anyone say anything to you during this that you didn't agree with? Or believe in?

DAVID: No, but no one's actually said the thing where I most agree with you, that writing can be like –

CAITLIN: No, it's literally a poo. These ideas all build up in your head and you'll go nuts if you don't get them out, and that's how you know you're going to be a writer. Although you know people do have different times of the day to write. I know that by half three I'm done. I don't think I've ever written anything good after half three. Unless I have to.

DAVID: Jon Ronson said he could write later in the day…

CAITLIN: But you don't want to. That's the other thing. Apart from writing being like a poo, which no one will ever talk about, it's a very bum-based job. Your arse hurts a lot if you're a journalist. There's no great writer in the world who has a really great arse. If you look through butt shots of Hemingway, Chandler, Parker, Brontë, you line them all up, they've got bums like trucks in a bad way. You are spending a lot of time on your bum, you have lower back problems like you would not believe. Your arse hurts a lot. That's why I would recommend buying a posturally correct stool. I pretend that mine is in fact a saddle on a horse, usually that of Artax in *The NeverEnding Story* and that when it gets difficult to write a piece, we're in the Slough of Despond and I'm just riding Artax going, 'Come on Artax, come on, you can make it,' and Artax is just gradually sinking in the sand. 'Come on Artax, we can make it out of here.' And sometimes we don't. Sometimes Artax dies and we have to knock it on the head and finish it the next day.

DAVID: That's the most unusual writing advice I've ever had.

CAITLIN: I'm really upset that the great writers never talk about this. There's no bum-based conversation from Tolstoy or Roth.

DAVID: Dickens wrote standing up.

CAITLIN: And that's how he wrote so many books. He stopped his vertebrae getting compacted. That's a huge factor. *Hard Arse* by Charles Dickens. *The Old Curiosity Arse*. But yeah beware of your arse. You can be in so much pain, particularly towards the end of a book. With screenwriters there's a reason nobody says, 'the beautiful posture and gait of a screenwriter.'

The conversation goes into a lot of details about posture and then, for some reason, facial symmetry. Perhaps significantly, it is Caitlin who wrests it back.

CAITLIN: But generally are you being cheerful about being a writer? Because I think it's a smashing job. I literally can't think of any more fun that you can have.

Caitlin then discusses her teenage hopes and dreams of hanging out at the Groucho Club with Fry & Laurie and how when she was thirteen she wrote to Lenny Henry to apply for the job of managing director of Comic Relief…

CAITLIN: And he wrote a really beautiful letter back a week later on Comic Relief headed notepaper, which was the single most valuable thing that had ever entered our postcode ever. It was from Lenny Henry, obviously seeing that I came from the Midlands and he's from the Midlands too, and it was like, 'Aw, thank you for your letter, baby, the fund's really boring but I'm sure we're going to see you flying like a comet through British society in the next ten years.'

And just one person going 'you can do it' – I wasn't getting it from anyone else. Literally the fact that he wrote me that letter was like, 'that means I can do it!' I think often as a writer you need to be given permission as well. If you're lucky enough to be middle class or upper class, I don't hate you, I'm not chippy, I've worked that out with a therapist, but this is for the working-class kids out there: no one's going to come and say to you 'come and be a writer'. You are going to have to push your way there and that's why whenever I do events or meet people and stuff and I see anybody who wants to be a writer I say to them, 'You can do it! I'm literally telling you now, I give you permission to be a writer.' 'Cos I think you do need someone to say to you, 'Yeah that's a valid choice.' You can do that.

And so I would echo that. You don't need anyone's permission to be a writer. But just in case you do, this book is that permission.

Afterword

And there we have it. Lots of interviews with lots of very different people. It struck me, reading these interviews back, what an immense variety of people is contained in these pages. The misfits, the confident ones, the artistic types, the workers: everyone different but everyone the same in one respect. They all know what it's like to be a writer (or, if we're being pedantic, what it's like to work with a writer).

Even though I knew that the men and women I spoke to for this book were very different, I don't think I realized just how different they would be. Some of them work early in the day, others late at night. Some like music, others can't work with it at all. Some of them draw their work from the deep well of the soul, others write according to what's been in the news that week. And all of them are driven by the need to write.

It's not the case that anyone can be a writer, but it is true that there are no barriers of class, identity and, most importantly, personality to being a writer. Jo Unwin's experiences of publishing and Catherine Rosenthal's knowledge of the financial issues show that it is very hard to exist as a writer (something which is a large part of the whole 'being' a writer business which is what I intended this book to be about).

And writing requires application. Suzanne Moore's columns, which emanate from her extraordinary mind, require constant reading and the ability to swim in the currents of modern life. Jon Ronson combines the slog of journalism and research with the kind of writing only Jon Ronson can do. Caitlin Moran takes the facts and experiences of her extraordinary life and makes them both funny and universal. Iszi Lawrence lives in a car and writes when everyone but Mark Billingham and Martyn Waites is asleep. Dennis Kelly and Emma Donoghue are powered by emotion and intelligence. Joel Morris and Jason Hazeley are surreal geniuses harnessed to the numbing practicalities of television. Mark Ellen is made of ideas.

Every writer, and every writer's experience, in this book is different. But they all go to show one thing, which is very like the old joke: an old lady is looking for a famous concert hall in New York. She approaches a policeman and asks him, 'Excuse me, officer, how do I get to Carnegie Hall?' And the cop says, 'Lady – ya gotta practise.'

How do you get to be a writer? It's easy.

You just have to write.

Mark Ellen's Favourite Things

After I'd spoken to Mark Ellen, I thought we'd covered every topic under and including the sun. But he was kind enough to send me a follow-up email. Mark wrote:

A few words and phrases I read and want to nick:

'Rhapsodic'

'A contrarian stunt'

'Mister Cameron to the Burns Unit!'

'Scream like a banshee if you disagree.'

'The best thing you could say about the place was at least the graffiti was spelt right.'

A few quotes and lyrics:

'Here we all are, sitting on a rainbow' – Small Faces in 'Lazy Sunday Afternoon'

'Man buys ring, woman throws it away/Same old thing happens every day' – McCartney in 'I'm Down'

'I like philosophy but optimism keeps busting in' – Dr Johnson

'The more I hear about him, the less I like him' – Rich Hall on Adolf Hitler

Some More Thoughts From Jason Hazeley

I love follow-up emails. Here's another, this time from Jason. He wrote:

There were a few tiny things I thought should have come out loud and didn't.

AGENT: Our agents do the bit we're bloody rubbish at, which is negotiating deals, getting contracts straight and chasing payment. All that stuff is poison to us. There comes a point once a year when I have to do my books for my accountant, and it enervates me beyond reason, because I think my accountant should be made to write five sketches in return. Fox and stork.

ALSO: Office politics terrify me. Because I haven't worked 'in an office' (even though I've literally sat in offices to work many times), I have no absolutely zero appreciation of office politics. I might as well be asked to write a poem in Danish using only my feet. As a result, I tend to get very David Mamet about it. 'You never open your mouth 'til you know what the shot is.' You only have to back the wrong horse and you're in danger of about fifty-five people thinking you're a dick.

EXCITES ME: Every bit of writing excites me. Starting it, finishing it, getting it right, getting it wrong, doing it well, struggling with it – all of it is great. And, because sketch writing often involves examining a specific area, we can often find ourselves going down research holes for several hours, all of which is great learning. We play a 'Today's Google searches' game occasionally (as does Sam Bain), and get these great confused salads of results like 'Dogging terminology', 'parts of the lung', 'Shostakovich', 'Touché Turtle'.

Just How Stoned Was Caitlin Moran?

CAITLIN: How stoned was I? At one point I was so stoned that I tried to see if I got a wasp stoned and I put it under a cup with a worm that wasn't stoned, if the worm would win.

By the same author